WHY DOCTORS DON'T GET RICH

BY TOM BURNS, MD

How YOU Can Create Freedom With Passive Income Investing

Charlie,

I'm so glad I met you!
Thanks for keeping me dressed
on Neiba, and thank for
the experienced life advice.

T. Bu

11TH STREET
PUBLISHING

Distributed by Eleventh Street Publishing
172 Center St.
Suite 202
Jackson, WY 83001

ISBN: 978-0-578-74482-7

First Edition

Praise for *Why Doctors Don't Get Rich*

If you have ever had dreams of financial freedom, this is a must read for you. Tom Burns has condensed a lifetime of experience and success into one book, so that you can achieve your dreams faster. Why Doctors Don't Get Rich *will give you the tools to create a wealthy mindset, make money work for you, and create the freedom to achieve success beyond money.*

—Gary Keller, CEO of Keller Williams Real Estate and author of
The One Thing

The hardest thing for smart people to do is ask for help...and when you do it's hard to know whom to trust. It's worse for doctors because every financial salesperson targets them...but doctors are so busy caring for patients, staying informed, and dealing with bureaucracy...there's little time to study fancy financial products. Thankfully, Dr. Tom Burns found the answer...and proved it by doing it in the real world. Tom's not only smart and accomplished, he's one of the few truly good guys. If you're a busy doctor (or know one) racing on a treadmill with no end in sight... read this book and let Tom Burns show you a better way.

—Russell Gray, Co-Host, *The Real Estate Guys Radio Show*

Tom Burn's is the real deal and the definition of the person who has it all. A practicing doctor, who loves what he does, loves his family, has an amazing lifestyle and has created financial independence through real estate and investing. Tom does a beautiful job sharing what has worked for him in his book Why Doctor's Don't Rich. *I highly recommend you get Tom's book and read it word for word and start your own path to having it all.*

—Kyle Wilson, Founder Jim Rohn International and KyleWilson.com

I only wish I had access to a book like this at the beginning of my law career. I can only image where I would be today. If you want to become financially educated, enjoy freedom of choice and live life with purpose, passion and service, this is a must read. Following the teachings of Rich Dad Poor Dad, Why Doctors Don't Get Rich *exposes doctors (and busy high-earning professionals) to the reality that there is more to financial life than working for a paycheck and falling into the trap of "the more you earn, the more you spend." Get out of the rat race. Work because you want to, not because you have to. I can't recommend this book enough.*

—**Mauricio J. Rauld, Esq., Premier Law Group Founder/CEO**

Dr. Burns has written a terrific story about how doctors like himself don't have to remain poor. Many of my clients, like Tom, are physicians who have discovered that the simple truths found in this book can allow them to build massive amounts of wealth while at the same time reducing their taxes by hundreds of thousands of dollars. A must read for anyone who loves their profession and is tired of not getting ahead, Tom reminds us that it's as much about our mindset about money as it is about the money itself.

—**Tom Wheelwright, Rich Dad Advisor, Tax Strategist and Author of *Tax-Free Wealth***

I have known way too many 'poor white collar' folks in my life, who work hard and make money but never become financially free. I've also worked with hundreds of millionaires as the founder of Capitalism.com, and I know that the way to get rich is to own assets. Tom's message in Why Doctor's Don't Get Rich *is essential for every person who is on the hamster wheel of income and wants to be free. Tom is a living example of someone who has built true financial freedom, which is why he is able to provide this amazing gift to the world. I have bought hundreds of copies for my friends, colleagues, and customers.*

—**Ryan Moran, Business Owner, Podcaster**

There's a massive paradigm shift going on and you can no longer operate as you once did to achieve the life you desire. That is precisely why I highly recommend this book for those looking for more security, joy and abundance in their life. Dr. Tom Burns takes you behind the scenes of what he did to achieve financial freedom, by laying out a powerful playbook for those who are looking for financial solutions you can implement immediately. This book will provide you with the specifics you need in order to create passive income so that you can regain the joy you once had as a physician and live life on your own terms. I don't think there's a better time for this book than now.

—John MacGregor, Rich Dad Advisor, CFP, Founder of ThrivePath: Financial Freedom Built to Last, Author of *The Top 10 Reasons the Rich Go Broke*

Many people, including doctors, are unaware that there are ways to create financial security other than their 401k. In Why Doctors Don't Get Rich, *Tom Burns helps you think like a wealthy person, then walks you through the process of how to become one. Read this book if you want to take control of your financial life.*

—Andy Tanner, Rich Dad Advisor, Speaker and Author of *401(k)aos and Stock Market Cash Flow*

Tom Burns is one of the happiest people I know because he's found a way to control his financial condition rather than have his financial condition control him. Why Doctors Don't Get Rich *is a road map to how Tom found his financial freedom, and how you can find yours, too! By learning Tom's methodology, you'll learn ways to make your money work for you instead of you working endlessly for money. It's a simple concept that takes time and effort to put into practice. Few have as much practice, experience and happiness as Tom Burns does.*

—Dana Samuelson, President, American Gold Exchange

The surest path to financial freedom is the creation of passive income. It has worked for me and thousands of others. Why Doctors Don't Get Rich *gives you the mindset of a financially free person, then gives you the steps to achieve your goals. This is a must read for anyone who wants to create passive income and live a life in which they can make their own choices*

—Ken McElroy, Rich Dad Advisor, Real Estate Entrepreneur, Educator and Author of *The ABC's of Real Estate*

Thank goodness Tom Burns, America's top surgeon/investor, has leveled the playing field; arming doctors with the knowledge, resources and mindset to actively enjoy the work they love while passively earning the financially-free lifestyle they deserve. The insights Tom shares from his decades of success are literally worth millions in excess income and years of extra time. This book is the key to happiness, wealth and freedom that every busy medical professional dreams of—we prescribe reading it from cover to cover STAT!

—Adam Taggart and Chris Martenson, Authors of *Prosper* and Founders of *Peak Prosperity*

Dr. Burns packed this book full of success recipes for the busy professional! His specific examples of the medical profession are truly impactful, and just as applicable to the attorney, plumber and college student working nights as a waiter. The lessons are relevant and simple to adopt. It is clear that his years of close friendship with Robert Kiyosaki helped Tom master the same art of communicating complex financial concepts in easy to understand terms that made Rich Dad, Poor Dad *so successful. Tom Burns has written a fantastic book that is a must read for anyone searching for a higher quality, more financially free life. Read it and take action today!*

—Gary Pinkerton, Veteran, Author, Real Estate Entrepreneur and Wealth Strategist

I pay close attention to folks who are successful in the subject they are teaching, and Tom is a living example of what can be done in his world. Study this book and use it as your guide to the life you thought was impossible.

—**Dave Zook, Author, Investor and Syndicator**

As physicians, we have a lot to read and a lot coming at us. Dr. Burns' book serves as a critical instruction manual that merges the perspective of a forward-thinking physician investor, who understands doctors, with the perspective of an investor who has interpreted market moves and learned from each cycle. The key is to build equity in yourself and Why Doctors Don't Get Rich *provides excellent insight into the process.*

—**Dr. Thomas Black, Founder of Napali Capital and Author of *The Passive Income Physician***

As a busy professional, if you only have time to read one book this year… make sure it's Why Doctors Don't Get Rich. *Dr. Tom Burns shares lessons from a lifetime spent helping others achieve their dreams at the highest levels of medicine, sports and business, while building a multi-million-dollar real estate empire through the best and worst of times. Dr. Burns gives us the roadmap to reclaim our freedom no matter the circumstances…no more excuses.*

—**Christian Cascone, Tech Entrepreneur, Sustainable Developer and Award-Winning Producer**

Dr. Tom Burns isn't another author with regurgitated knowledge borrowed from academic study. Instead, he's a seasoned veteran of medicine and money. His unique story of how he found a way to practice medicine for the love of it, while using the tools inside this book to remove the need for money, will shake you to your core and disrupt everything you've been taught about financial freedom.

—**Damion Lupo, Founder of Black Belt Financial and Host of Financial Underdogs**

Dr. Tom Burns has cracked the code in helping doctors gain more freedom, meaning and joy in their lives. How? By showing doctors how to dramatically increase their passive income. Something they were never taught in medical school. Why Doctors Don't Get Rich fills in the blanks and provides deep insight about the importance of mindset and money. This step by step book is a life changing revelation for any doctor who wants to gain more fulfillment and peace in their life. If you crave the ability and choice to make a difference in yourself and the world…this is a must read!

—JW Wilson, Executive Director: The Learning Code Institute, Author of *Cracking The Learning Code*

"Driven" professionals aspire for a lifestyle that very few of them ever achieve because their wealth is their income, and trading their time is the only way to earn it. Tom Burns' book Why Doctor's Don't Get Rich not only demonstrates why trading time for money will never result in financial freedom, it gives you a playbook to escape the rat race and live the life of your dreams.

—Patrick Donohoe, Author of *Heads I Win, Tails You Lose*

Why Doctor's Don't Get Rich *is written from the perspective of a practitioner, someone in the trenches, who elevated himself from the financial dependence treadmill of surgeries, enabling him to practice medicine on his terms, for the love of it; all while building sustainable wealth. For any professional who is trapped in a gilded prison, Tom Burns shows the pathway out.*

—Victor Menasce, Author of *Magnetic Capital*

We all have a "little voice" in our head, our subconscious, that guides us to success or failure. Why Doctors Don't Get Rich *will train that voice for success and will give you actionable ideas to get you started. Tom Burns has done a masterful job of weaving thought and action into one indispensable resource to help you gain the freedom you desire.*

—Blair Singer, Best-Selling Author, Founder of Blair Singer Training Academy, Rich Dad Advisor

Tom has shared his life experiences and investment lessons in this great book. If you love being a physician and want to enjoy taking care of your patient's then you must read Why Doctors Don't Get Rich. *It will guide you on your path to lead a rich, healthy, wealthy life. Thank you, Tom.*

—**Carlos Ayala MD, FACS, Clinical Associate Professor UTRGV School of Medicine**

A must-read! Doctors and most other professionals are well educated academically and professionally, but not financially. It's just not part of our formal education system. Let this book be a guide on your journey to financial freedom.

—**Marco Santarelli, Host of *The Passive Real Estate Investing Podcast***

As a physician in the early stage of my career, I feel it is deeply imperative that practicing physicians understand the impact of the ideas presented by Tom Burns. Why Doctors Don't Get Rich *is positively industry-disrupting and life-altering for both physicians and patients.*

—**George Ozoude, Orthopedic Surgeon**

Why Doctors Don't Get Rich *is essential reading for physicians and other professionals. It is a clear and practical book featuring positive attitudes for success and wealth.*

—**Garrett Sutton, Rich Dad Advisor, Attorney and Author of *Own Your Own Corporation***

Success is about more than titles, degrees and income. Real success comes from figuring out your unique gifts and passions to accomplish your personal goals while serving as an example to others. In a nutshell, that is who Tom Burns is, and it becomes vividly clear in the pages of this excellent book. In Why Doctors Don't Get Rich, *Tom not only helps doctors and other high-income professionals develop the mindset of an investor, but he outlines practical steps and real-world insights that will help propel you to a richer more satisfying future. Don't waste another minute…this book is just what the doctor ordered!*

—**Robert Helms, Host of *The Real Estate Guys Radio Show***

Acknowledgments

To my wife, Phoebe, for putting up with my writing obsession; Robert Kiyosaki for the inspiration to write the book and for his decades of teaching; JW Wilson and David Bauer-Ray for guidance and heart; Kyle Wilson for always keeping me on the right path; Gary Keller for advice on how to write a good book; Garrett Sutton and Tom Wheelwright for graciously providing expert content; Matthew Gilbert, Christa Bourg and Sandy Draper for thoughtful editing; Joni McPherson for layout and cover expertise; John MacGregor for advice and guidance; Gabriel Petty for allowing me to drone on about financial independence for ten years; all the friends, too numerous to list, who were kind enough to read the rough drafts and give thoughtful feedback; and finally, my business partner, Darin Davis, and the team at Presario Ventures, for allowing me to take time from the business to pursue my mission and write this book.

With deep gratitude,

Tom

TABLE OF CONTENTS

Author's Note..xvii

Foreword   Robert Kiyosaki.............................. xix

Part I — What is a Rich Doctor?........................ 1

Chapter 1   Rich Dad and a Random Car Wash 3

Chapter 2   Why Do We Need Rich Doctors? 9
             How We Got Here............................ 10
             My Story................................... 12
             What's in it for You? 16

Part II — How to Think Like a Rich Doctor 19

Chapter 3   Why Do You Want to be Rich? 21
             Find Your Why 22
             What is Rich.............................. 24
             Defining True Wealth....................... 26
             Inner and Outer Wealth..................... 28
             Are Doctors Rich?......................... 29
             Wealth is a State of Mind 31

Chapter 4   Develop a Rich Mindset 35
             The Power of Thought 35
             Money Is Only a Tool...................... 36
             Reign in Your Ego......................... 37
             Cultivate Humility 39
             Have a Positive Attitude.................... 39
             Mind Your Words 41
             Develop Discipline and Good Habits............ 42
             Set Goals................................. 43
             Create Focus 45
             Develop Persistence 46
             Always Be Growing......................... 46

Chapter 5 **Get a Rich Education**........................ 49

Traditional Education vs. Wealth Education......... 50

Become a Reader................................. 51

Attend Seminars 53

Don't Fear Mistakes 54

Learn to Sell.................................... 56

Grow Your Network 57

Chapter 6 **Know the Rules of the Game** 61

Who is Grading You? 62

The Financial Statement.......................... 62

It's How You Make Your Money that Counts 64

Turning Point................................... 66

Beware the Wall Street Mystique 67

Average Returns 69

Ask Your Hairdresser 70

Ninety to Nothing............................... 71

Know Your Options 72

Bad Guys in Disguise 73

Doctor Watch Your Back 74

Money Doesn't Play Favorites 75

Chapter 7 **Understand Money, Inflation, and Hard Assets**... 77

The Dollar Decline 77

Inflation 79

Four Asset Types................................ 82

Why Hard Assets?............................... 88

Explore Your Options............................ 89

Chapter 8 **Get in the Game** 91

Start with Baby Steps 92

Find Your Niche 93

Seek Mentors................................... 94

Find Partners 95

Seek Associations 96

Bucket of Crabs................................. 97

Part III — How to Become a Rich Doctor 99

Chapter 9 **Make Money Work for You** 101
Trading Time for Money 102
The Power of Passive Income 103
The Magic Formula. 104
Remote Income 107
Multiple Streams of Income. 108
Where Do You Find Passive Income? 108
Buckets and Pipelines. 109
Choices and Control. 109

Chapter 10 **Cash Flow Is King** 113
Net Worth vs. Cash Flow 114
Cash Flow vs. Capital Gain 115
Is Capital Gain Bad? 116
Weathering the Storms. 117
Define Your Expenses. 119
Beware of the Consumer Trap. 120
The Velocity of Money 121
Chasing Home Runs. 122

Chapter 11 **The Magic of Leverage** 125
Financial Leverage 126
Bad Debt. 127
Good Debt 128
Time Leverage 129
Knowledge Leverage. 130
Experience Leverage. 131
Relationship Leverage. 132
Technology Leverage 133
Teamwork. 134
Creating Your Team 135
Syndication 136

Chapter 12 **Protect Your Stuff**. 139
Separate Your Assets. 140

Limit Your Losses 141
Own Nothing but Control Everything. 142
Legal Documents 144
Protect Your Children's Future 145
Beyond Asset Protection 146
Expert Advice—Garrett Sutton, Esq. 146

Chapter 13   Keep More of Your Money 153
Legally Avoiding Taxes. 154
Partner with the Government 155
Doctors and Taxes. 157
Next Steps. 159
Expert Advice—Tom Wheelwright, CPA 160

Chapter 14   Fundamentals and Guidelines 165
Passive vs. Active Investing 166
Passive Investing with a Sponsor 168
What Makes a Good Sponsor? 170
What Makes a Good Investment?. 173
Tax Time as an Investor 176
Third-party Review. 177

Chapter 15   Choose Your Vehicle 179
Real Estate 179
Business Ownership 183
Paper Assets. 185
Gold 186
Oil and Gas 187
Agriculture. 188
Insurance 188
Art. 189
Philanthropy 190
Other Tools 190
Be an Insider 190

Conclusion   Build a Pipeline to Your Dreams 193

Author's Note

As a doctor, you spend twelve hours a day getting chewed up, spit out and often treated like a commodity while trying to provide quality care to people in need. After that you are expected to go home exhausted and be a model spouse or parent. For some of you, that burden has become too great and you are looking for a way out. My mission is to make sure you never feel like that again.

Many of you enjoy life as a doctor, but would like more security, more time, and the freedom to practice medicine on your own terms. This book will help you achieve that goal.

I wrote this as a roadmap for people who want more from life than a job and a paycheck—it's for those who want a life of freedom, joy and purpose. Isn't that what we all want? The first step is to not be dependent on that paycheck.

I've compressed almost three decades of investment and life experience into this one source so that you can learn from my wins and losses, and achieve your goals as fast as possible. This book will give you the tools and mindset to turn your salary into lifelong passive income. When you accomplish that, you will create a life in which you have choices and control over what you do. That is freedom.

With that freedom, some physicians will exit medicine, but others will use it to create a more compassionate system. I fully believe that, when relieved of financial stress, many will use their time and passion to drive innovation and relieve suffering. That can change the world.

The book is just the start. The living, breathing organism will be the community at www.richdoctor.com. There these concepts will be constantly expanded and refined to bring you the most up-to-date information that will help you create passive income. It will be a hub where experts from all over the world will provide guidance and expertise to support your journey. The most efficient way to reach your goals faster is to use the book and the website in combination.

What you are about to read is the foundation of what created my personal financial independence and it will work for you. I wish you an exciting journey!

Tom

Foreword

By Robert Kiyosaki

T om Burns is a special friend. Not only is Dr. Burns a leader in financial education for the medical profession, he is a kind and generous human being. The world needs more leaders like Tom Burns and that is why I am happy to write this Foreword for a friend, teacher, entrepreneur, and medical doctor.

On April 8, 1997 I self-published *Rich Dad Poor Dad*. The book had to be self-published because it was rejected by every New York publishing house. On a few rejection slips, editors added personal comments such as, "When it comes to money, you don't know what you're talking about."

The editors objected to my rich dad's lessons on money; lessons such as:

1. "The rich do not work for money."

Today, nearly 25 years after my book was published, many more people are aware of the growing gap between the haves and the have nots in America. Simply put, the rich are people who do not work for money. The poor and middle class are people who do work for money.

2. "Your house is not an asset."

The book publishing house editors really went wild on this lesson. For millions of people, owning a home is a quasi-religious experience. In 2007, 10 years after *Rich Dad Poor Dad* was published, after the subprime mortgage disaster nearly brought down the world economy, millions found out the hard way that their home is not an asset.

3. "Savers are losers."

This lesson really got to them, too. For many people, saving money is the bedrock of financial intelligence. Most people subscribe to Benjamin Franklin's words of wisdom, *"A penny saved is a penny earned."* That may have been true in 1737, when Ben wrote those words in his book Poor Richard's Almanac, but they are not true today. After the 2008 crash, millions of savers became losers as the Federal Reserve Bank began printing trillions of dollars and lowering interest rates to zero and below. ZIRP (zero interest rate policy) and printing money caused savers to become the biggest losers.

Today, millions believe in living "debt free." In reality, debt can make you rich—if you know how to use it. And that requires financial education. Without real financial education, debt—consumer debt—makes the poor and middle class poorer.

In 1997, when no one wanted *Rich Dad Poor Dad*, I called a friend in Austin, Texas, and asked if he would put my book in his car wash. He (like everyone else) said "No," adding: "We don't sell books in car washes."

After a bit of arm twisting, using our years of friendship as a lever, he finally agreed to put two dozen books on sale, in his car wash, on consignment. He warned me: "If they don't sell, you're getting them back."

For a week I pestered him, asking if any books had been sold. The answer was always the same, "No. No one wants your book."

The following week, I called my friend again. "You won't believe it," he said. "All your books are gone."

"Do you want any more?" I asked.

"No," he said. "I told you, we don't sell books in car washes."

Two years after the first two dozen books were sold, Oprah Winfrey called and I flew to Chicago to be on Oprah! On that day, my book and I went from unknown to world famous.

Since the humble beginnings in a car wash in Austin, Texas, *Rich Dad Poor Dad* has sold over 41 million copies. *Rich Dad Poor Dad* was on *The New York Times* bestseller list for nearly seven years. Today, *Rich Dad Poor Dad* is the number one personal finance book of all time.

For years, I wondered who bought those first books…

In 2018, Tom and I were both instructors at The Real Estate Guys' Summit at Sea cruise. One evening Tom and I began talking about the book and the car wash. I did not realize that he bought the first *Rich Dad* book—and that the book was still in his possession.

Tom returned that book—the first copy of *Rich Dad Poor Dad* ever sold—to me and today it is proudly displayed in my office in Phoenix.

That is why Dr. Tom Burns is a very special friend and fellow teacher, bringing financial education to the world.

This is why I whole heartedly support Tom's book and his work as a medical doctor, friend, teacher, investor, entrepreneur, and all-around good guy.

Robert Kiyosaki

PART I

What is a Rich Doctor?

The greatness of a man is not how much wealth he acquires, but in his integrity and his ability to affect those around him positively.

—Bob Marley

Chapter 1

Rich Dad and a Random Car Wash

Fortune favors the prepared mind.

– Louis Pasteur

T he day started without much excitement and provided no promise of anything different. 1997 was halfway in the bag and the Texas heat was brutal. I was doing some routine errands around Austin and my most pressing goal was to get out of the sun. Little did I know that my life was about to change forever.

My truck was dusty and needed cleaning, so I pulled into the local car wash. I handed the attendant my keys and went inside to get out of the heat and pay the bill. While my vehicle was running through the brushes, I handed the cashier my credit card and noticed several copies of a book, loosely stacked on the counter behind her, with a hand-written "For Sale" sign next to them. I found it strange that a car wash would sell books, but I was an avid reader, and it had an interesting title with a flashy purple and yellow cover. I thought the title, *Rich Dad Poor Dad*, was clever, so I asked her to add it to my bill.

When I got home, I dumped the book on my office desk and went about my day. That night, at about 11:30, I passed my office on the way to bed and remembered the book. I opened the front cover and read a few sentences from Chapter 1. It was interesting, so I decided to read a page or two more before turning in. After several more pages, I sat down and continued to read. About four hours later, I had finished the entire book.

My mind was racing. Prior to that night, I knew I wanted cash flow and had been on a quest to understand money, freedom and lifestyle. What I had just read crystallized previously amorphous thoughts and gave me clarity. I now understood why I wanted passive income and how it would create my financial freedom. I needed to tell somebody, but it was 3:30 a.m. and everybody I knew was asleep. I impatiently waited until 7 o'clock and called a friend, telling him I had just finished the best book I had ever read.

I gave him my copy a few days later and he finished it the same day. He called the number on the publishing page, wanting to find out where we could get more books. To his surprise, the voice on the other end of the line belonged to the author, Robert Kiyosaki. He was just as surprised as my friend.

Apparently, the book was self-published and only 1,000 copies were printed. Sales were not expected to be brisk and the car wash only had two dozen. The book I took home that afternoon turned out to be the very first copy sold! The next day I bought what was left at the car wash. My friend claimed Robert's remaining stock and planned to distribute them through the Amway organization.

In short order, a dozen of us had read the book and we quickly bought airline tickets to meet Robert and his wife, Kim, in Scottsdale, Arizona. Robert taught us how to play Cashflow, his financial education board game. He explained that *Rich Dad Poor Dad* was first designed as a brochure to help sell the game. My wife won, and her prize was to keep Robert's game. (We are still proud owners of one of the first editions!)

We finished our visit in Scottsdale and returned home with a mission. I wanted my friends to know about this book. It changed my life and I wanted it to change theirs. Soon, the rest of the world would discover its value.

Rich Dad Poor Dad would go on to become one of the best-selling personal finance books ever written with an estimated 40 million copies now in print worldwide! Robert and I became good friends. My life was never the same.

Flash forward 20 years…

It's early morning and I am sitting outside, overlooking Culebra Bay on the Papagayo Peninsula in Costa Rica, enjoying a cup of local coffee. From the deck of our villa, I can see fishermen and tourist boats heading to the nearby hotel. A *coatimundi*, Central America's version of a raccoon, is keeping his eye on me from the edge of the infinity pool. I soak in the beautiful morning light and am aware of being at peace.

I reflected on how 12 months before I'd been on an ice shelf in Antarctica, watching seals, penguins and orcas, then jumping into the coldest water I had ever experienced. I had spent two weeks in Africa, four weeks in Colorado, nine days on a cruise ship in the Caribbean, two weeks in the Canadian wilderness, a week in Mexico, and another four weeks at various places across the country. The following week, I was flying to Phoenix to attend a three-day Mastermind Workshop on personal growth. And throughout all this, I wasn't worried about missing work.

Doesn't everyone dream of some version of this lifestyle? My passion is travel, but for you, it might be playing golf or spending more time with your family. What's important is that you can have the life you desire if you focus on a plan to get there. My journey was made possible by what you'll learn in this book. I've spent tens of thousands of hours learning how to create this lifestyle and I have invested a fortune to learn from dozens of the world's experts. It has been an awesome journey and now I have distilled that experience into one easy-to-read source for you.

You see, I'm a doctor, and all doctors are rich and happy, right? Wrong! Today, we see a constant stream of stories about long hours, physician burnout, suicide and disenchantment with our profession. The changes in medicine have led to an epidemic of unhappy, unfulfilled, and fed up physicians. Many doctors feel trapped and don't know what to do.

The good news is that it doesn't have to be that way. You can enjoy your life now and create the freedom to design your future.

A Life Less Typical

I have a thriving practice, but I'm not your typical physician. I've learned to work less, travel more, and still keep control of my life. I now practice orthopedic surgery because I enjoy it, not because I need the money. This remarkable shift in mindset has made a substantial positive difference in my relationships with my family and patients. I am writing this book because you deserve the same chance to create *your* ideal life.

Of course, I still have daily challenges and life isn't perfect. However, what affords me this lifestyle is not the fact that I am a doctor. What sets me apart is my financial education and the fact that I created *passive income*, which produces money whether I work or not. My passive income pays for the life I *want* to live—not the one I *have* to live— because of the principles that I am about to share with you. Your ideal life is possible if you're willing to open your mind.

If you still have a passion for your profession, these principles will enable you to enjoy that passion. If you are feeling burned out, they might bring you back to your original life purpose. If you're ready to leave your job, they can help you do that. I wrote this book because I want to share what has worked for me and can work for you.

My passive income pays for the life I WANT to live—
not the one I HAVE to live.

Getting Here

How did I get here? Over 30 years ago, after 26 years of formal education, I realized that I had never been taught about money. I knew history, science, math and how to fix a knee, but no one had ever taught me how to become wealthy. I decided to educate myself about passive income or what some call "mailbox money."

I went to seminars, read hundreds of books, and found great people who acted as mentors. But, most importantly, I acted! I didn't wait until I had all the answers. I dove into the game as soon as I saw an opening. I knew that merely trading my time for money by stacking my days with surgeries wouldn't take me where I wanted to go. If I kept doing that, I would just be a "poor doctor" with money. I wanted to be a "rich doctor" with choices.

That should make me unique, right? Hardly. If I was that special, I would have been more successful and found my freedom much earlier. I was plagued by ego, fear, uncertainty and a busy schedule. Luckily, the financial education I sought outside of medicine gave me the tools to fight those obstacles and keep moving forward.

All I did was follow a simple plan and never quit learning. I made boatloads of mistakes, but slowly the victories outweighed the defeats and I started winning the game. Those victories then provided me the opportunity to hang out with other winners.

Today I have friends from across the world who share my passions and my freedom. Most are entrepreneurs; many are in real estate; all are givers and teachers.

Arguably, my best teacher has been Robert Kiyosaki, and the story of our first meeting was chronicled above. We've been friends for over 20 years, and I'm always learning something new. He has positively impacted the lives of countless people across the globe, yet he still teaches. Occasionally, I'm privileged to gather with him and other like-minded folks to study together. We talk about *real* wealth, which revolves around giving, spirituality, and relationships. If those are internalized, the money usually follows.

I want everyone to have mental and financial freedom. Imagine your world if you didn't have to count exclusively on the revenue from your medical practice. Imagine the experience your patients would have. Wouldn't it be fantastic not to have to overbook your schedule to create revenue? Wouldn't it be wonderful to enjoy medicine for the noble profession that it is? Wouldn't it be great to have the time and money to explore your wildest dreams?

I primarily talk about physicians in this book because that is my world, but they are the perfect avatar for professionals everywhere. The same principles will work equally well for anyone with a steady income and a desire for more freedom and control of their life. What better way to improve the health and wellbeing of society than to have professionals who are freed from escalating financial constraints and able to embrace a mission of good? So, wherever you see the word "doctor" in this book, insert your job or profession and continue down the road to financial freedom.

And just to be clear, this isn't a "get rich quick" scheme or a specific roadmap to your individual success. Instead, you'll discover a set of principles that, if applied, will work every time. And while I said that this formula was simple, I didn't say it was easy. There is a lot of humility, personal growth, and paradigm shift involved, so if you feel you must always be the smartest person in the room, this book may not be for you. It will require some changes and some work on yourself. But if you can commit, it's an investment that will pay off.

Wherever you see the word "doctor" in this book, insert your job or profession and continue down the road to financial freedom.

I won't guarantee that it's all here, but if you're genuinely searching for answers, this book can help you get more out of life, so dive in! My sincerest hope is that I will awaken the entrepreneur or financial genius in you. If I've done that, I will have reached my goal: To serve you so that you can create the life you desire. I want you to be a "rich doctor" with all that implies. Let the journey begin!

Chapter 2

Why Do We Need Rich Doctors?

The two most important days in your life are the day you are born and the day you find out why.

—MARK TWAIN

I hopped into my truck, exhausted but confident I'd found my calling. I had just left a steakhouse where I had given a talk to roughly thirty physicians about medicine, money, and real estate. The reason I was so worn out is that most of them had kept my team and me there, asking questions for two hours after the program was over!

Why would thirty busy doctors make time on a Monday night to listen to someone talk about money and freedom? They were there because today, physicians are trapped in a profession they love but a business they hate. Those at the dinner were looking for answers to solve that dichotomy. They were hungry for knowledge and were searching for answers to create a more joyful and balanced life. I had found my mission.

Today, physicians are trapped in a profession they love but a business they hate.

You see, as physicians, we were never taught to be rich. We were taught to be "poor." Let me explain. Poor doctors spend what they make, and while they live well enough, they can never stop working. Through no fault of their own, their high-level education was designed to mold them into doctors, not make them rich.

While most of the folks in that room were probably great physicians (and might have had big bank accounts), the world of real wealth creation was new to them. They hadn't yet learned how to think like "rich doctors"—doctors who have learned how to make money work *for* them. A rich doctor is financially educated, enjoys freedom of choice, and lives life with purpose, passion and service. This group wanted that freedom—don't we all?

So, we spent the balance of the night fielding questions about control and creating passive income. There were comments like, "I didn't know you could do that!" or "I felt so trapped until I heard you speak." The energy was electric! This group made a good living, but they were frustrated and wanted true work-life balance. Most people perceive doctors as rich, but the personal cost of that reputation is negatively affecting them and the patients they treat.

How We Got Here

In medical school, I had no concept of physician income. I knew doctors did well but had no real sense of the numbers until after graduation. My first exposure was at a meeting in 1987 when I was doing my orthopedic training at a hospital in Cincinnati.

We were at our morning conference when, suddenly, we heard this rumble that sounded like an earthquake. I was from Texas and didn't know if earthquakes occurred in Ohio, so I asked what was going on. The older physician leading the discussion said, "Oh, that's Dr. so-and-so with his new hotrod." More specifically, it was a twin-turbocharged Porsche 959 that was barely street-legal, had to be special ordered, and cost ten times my annual resident salary! That certainly gave me hope for my financial future.

We all know things have changed in recent years. Healthcare costs eventually outpaced inflation and then got out of control. As a result, physicians have come under constant financial and administrative attacks.

Insurance companies have become for-profit entities that squeeze every penny they can. The doctors are now the weakest link in this medical ecosystem, and they are at the mercy of insurance companies, hospitals, and large, corporate-run physician organizations. Physician reimbursement, adjusted for inflation, declines every year. At the same time, expenses continue to rise organically with inflation. This increase in expenses is worsened by requirements for costly software and the ever-increasing numbers of employees required to keep up with government regulations and to manage insurance forms.

This margin contraction has led to consolidation in the industry. Many physicians are now employees of large organizations or hospitals. This was supposed to create efficiency, but instead, it is affecting doctor-patient relationships and eroding salaries. Corporations and boards are making the decisions, not the doctor who is taking care of the patient.

This is creating a high level of job dissatisfaction among physicians. Comments I've read include, "You are supposed to just feel warm and fuzzy knowing you helped mankind . . . hopefully, not spending retirement living in a cardboard box under a bridge somewhere." Another physician lamented, "All that paperwork sucks the enjoyment out of being a doctor."[1]

Physician burnout is at an all-time high and hovers around 50 percent.[2] This means that half of the doctors out there have wanted to quit medicine at one time or another—and maybe still do. The reasons for this crisis are many: crushing student debt, increasing bureaucratic tasks, too many hours at work, burdensome electronic medical records, decreasing reimbursements, and lack of control and autonomy. For all these reasons, many physicians consider leaving the field of medicine. Others state they would like to stay if they can find a way to improve their situation.

Physicians basically give up the third decade of their life training for their profession. The education is expensive, and many are saddled with student debt that averages $200,000.[3] This creates immediate financial and life stress. I recently spoke with an orthopedic surgeon on the West Coast who carried a $400,000 debt from his training. That would take most physicians years to pay off. My daughter just finished a pediatric residency with 34 other doctors. All had loan obligations.

Not only are new doctors saddled with enormous debt, but physician reimbursement is also flat or even declining when indexed to inflation. Today, medical students are paying the most ever for their education while entering a field where the income is going down.

Although physician incomes are stagnant, we still make an above-average professional living. However, control is being ceded to more powerful entities. Unless the system reverses course, doctors may become powerless cogs in a giant, corporate healthcare machine.

If we can't dismantle the burdensome infrastructure and oversight that has infected medicine over the past 20 years, we must reinvent ourselves. The good news is that you can take charge of your own destiny, and that's what this book is about.

As a doctor who is less dependent on income from medicine, you will have more latitude and more control over how you practice. This will produce a more pleasant and caring environment for your patients. You may still work within the same system, but you'll be able to eliminate or alter conditions that negatively affect your time, your income, and your patients' care and experience in the office.

As you gain control of your financial and professional environment, your life will transform. This will create a better life for you and your family while your patients will benefit from your lack of stress. Your freedom, compassion and purpose will have a positive effect on those whose lives you touch—and the ripple effect might change the world for the better. That's why we need "rich doctors."

A rich doctor is financially educated, enjoys freedom of choice, and lives life with purpose, passion and service.

My Story

I had a great childhood and grew up neither rich nor poor. My father was a Secret Service agent whose job was to take a bullet for presidents and visiting dignitaries. My mother was a nurse. Neither was entrepreneurial; the closest my dad got to the investment world was to lose half of his savings in his best friend's failed restaurant venture. It turned out that good wine and linguini could not overcome lousy management and an average location.

I stayed out of law enforcement and went into sports medicine as an orthopedic surgeon. During my training, I began to get closer to the surgeons who were in private practice. They weren't all happy.

Although they were making staggering (inflation-adjusted) incomes compared to today, there were constant complaints about reimbursement cuts, insurance issues, and lack of time with family. They were losing control of their profession and they didn't know what to do. Sure, they were making hefty sums of money, but their incomes and lifestyles were under attack by forces they didn't command.

I was beginning to think about life after training and didn't want to become stressed and unhappy like many of the doctors I was observing. I needed answers, so I started to research medicine in general and its potential future over the next forty years.

I discovered a system in which the real power resided in the C-suites. Insurance companies were constructing HMOs and other products designed to decrease the cost of medicine, but in reality they reduced pay, diluted autonomy, and eroded doctor/patient relationships.

Physicians were starting to be told how much they would get paid and were saddled with increasing amounts of paperwork in addition to their clinical duties. I decided not to put myself at the mercy of a system I felt was preparing to attack my profession. I needed to develop some sort of income that wasn't correlated with the medical industry.

Like most doctors, I was never given financial training, either in college or medical school, but I knew I had to learn. I began to read everything I could and soon became more aware of the financial world. This eventually led me to real estate investing, which was perfect for me. It was simple, understandable, and the barrier to entry was low. Real estate provided passive income, tax advantages, and a hedge against inflation. It could also be done part-time, outside of office hours and on weekends, and with or without partners. This fit the life of a full-time surgeon.

I started with small projects in the mid-to-late 1990s, made plenty of mistakes, and learned lots of lessons. Some of the projects were successful and overall there were more wins than losses.

Eventually, I got to a point where I wanted to expand my knowledge. I had a good friend who had been very successful in real estate and I asked him if he would teach me what he knew. He was kind enough to let me work with him for several years. During this "apprenticeship," through time management and sheer will, I maintained a full-time orthopedic surgery practice. There was no compensation for my real estate work.

While this seems like a poor return for an orthopedic surgeon to work for someone else without pay, that relationship gave me a priceless education and eventually led to the development of a multimillion-dollar medical office complex. My friend and I remain close and I am still learning.

During this time, I also continued to follow the conventional wisdom of buying a balanced portfolio of stocks, bonds, and mutual funds. This was reinforced by the rising stock market, enthusiastic TV pundits, and my broker friends. Like many others, my portfolio got killed in the dot-com crash in 2001.

By the time 2008 rolled around, I'd learned some new lessons. The stock and bond markets had been rising along with housing prices. A little voice in my head started nagging me and I took all my money out of equities before the Great Recession and the ensuing market crash. That saved my meager stock portfolio.

What I didn't appreciate was the general economy is tightly interconnected with the stock markets and that relationship was about to severely affect my life. By this time, I had progressed from private investing to putting deals together for investors. In a heartbeat, the capital markets dried up, and I had guaranteed loans that became due. For the first time in my life, I owed people money and I didn't immediately have the cash to pay them back. I was mortified.

My reputation was more important to me than the money, so over the next two years I took out multiple lines of credit, sold our family lake house, and used all my personal cash to ensure that all my investors were paid dollar for dollar, plus interest.

It was a painful time, emotionally and financially. As a husband and father, I was embarrassed that our lifestyle had to be limited. In addition, that was the start of the greatest real estate boom in modern history. Because I lacked readily available cash, I was unable to take advantage of the spectacular deals available. However, it was the right thing to do, and I kept my credibility with my investors. Some years later, those relationships would turn out to be profitable.

In addition to my budding real estate career, I tried all sorts of ventures from the mid-1990s to the Great Recession looking for the right formula for financial success. I joined Amway. I invested in medical and non-medical businesses. Despite the difficulty my father had experienced, I owned and ran a restaurant. I built, syndicated, and co-founded a full-service hospital. I even spent a year as the marketing director for a magnetic lighter company.

Some of these efforts failed economically, but the experiences weren't failures. In each venture, I learned a lesson that helped me become wiser and more resilient.

Multilevel marketing taught me about sales, personal development, and how to overcome the fear of failure. The companies I invested in taught me the importance of management. The stock market taught me that it's best to have control over your investments. The lighter company taught me about sales and distribution. Restaurant ownership taught me about service, marketing and margins. The hospital business taught me how to manage hundreds of employees and introduced me to the power of the government.

These lessons have served me well, helping me to be successful enough in real estate to make my income as a physician unnecessary. It has been a long ride, but the education isn't over. To this day, I attend multiple seminars each year, read as many books as I can, and focus my efforts on providing value for my investors. I continue to practice orthopedic surgery, but on my own terms and I still enjoy it. I have the best of both worlds, and you can too!

What's in it for You?

You might feel medicine is a calling, or maybe you can't wait to get out? Money isn't the answer to everything, but it can give you options. If it's your goal to exit medicine, these principles can help you get there. If you still enjoy the healing, you can craft your medical life so that it's in harmony with the reasons that first drew you to medicine. To do this in the most efficient way, it helps to have a guide.

My mission is to be that guide and help you transform your personal and professional life. This book will give you the tools to build a pipeline, flowing with passive income, that bridges the gap between where you are now and where you want to be in your future. We will build that pipeline together.

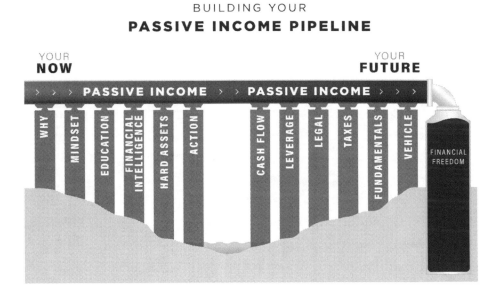

BUILDING YOUR
PASSIVE INCOME PIPELINE

With each successive chapter, we will build the structure that supports your pipeline. Each pillar that holds up your pipeline represents a simple, yet effective concept that reinforces your flow of passive income. These lessons are distilled from my 25 years of experience, and were learned the hard way through mistakes, trial and error, and constant education.

These principles will help you to avoid taking the long road to financial freedom—like I did. A well-constructed pipeline of passive income will relieve some financial pressure and give you the freedom to create the life you always dreamed of.

My wish is for every doctor to read this book. And then for every lawyer, engineer, and salesman—really, every professional of any kind—to do so as well. The mission is to have an army of people who are financially free and can change the world.

Some may wish to retire early to enjoy their lives, while others will want to continue in their chosen profession but with less stress and interference. Still, others will pour their energies into something new, like curing cancer or making life better for others.

Hopefully, the knowledge I have gained as an active entrepreneur can help you reach your goals—whatever they are. And if more people like you are working and living on their own terms, won't that make this world a better, happier place?

The transformation begins in your mind.

PART II

How to Think Like a Rich Doctor

To achieve something you have never done before, you must become somebody you have never been before.

—LES BROWN

BUILDING YOUR
PASSIVE INCOME PIPELINE

YOUR
NOW

YOUR
FUTURE

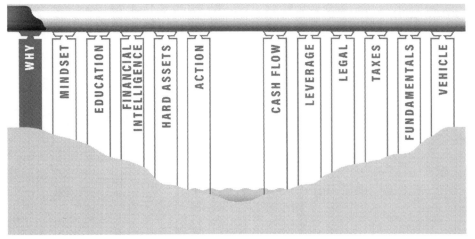

WHY · MINDSET · EDUCATION · FINANCIAL INTELLIGENCE · HARD ASSETS · ACTION · CASH FLOW · LEVERAGE · LEGAL · TAXES · FUNDAMENTALS · VEHICLE

Chapter 3

Why Do You Want to be Rich?

There are people who have money and people who are rich.

—Coco Chanel

L et's start with a question only you can answer: Why did you become a doctor?

Having been a physician for 34 years, I've heard most of the reasons. Some had a seminal medical event that implanted the desire to become a doctor. Others were influenced by another medical professional that they, in turn, wanted to emulate. Many simply wanted to help others and realized that medicine is one of the noblest ways to do that. That white coat and the prestige of the "Doctor" title recruited quite a few as well. Personally, I was an athlete who wasn't good enough to get paid for it, so I chose orthopedic surgery to remain close to the athletes I admired and wanted to hang out with.

These are just a few of the many valid reasons to become a physician. Rarely in my travels have I run across a doctor who got into it for the money. While we know there is some surety of financial reward, there are other less time-consuming ways to make money, and very few of us would put that reason as number one.

Whatever reason you chose to enter medicine is uniquely yours and is the reason *WHY* you are a doctor. For me, it was the driving force that kept me going during college and medical school. It was the reward I visualized when I had to study reams of seemingly worthless information to pass a pharmacology test in medical school. It was what got me out of bed when I was on call and hadn't slept for 24 hours, yet I had to survive another caffeine-fueled day in the hospital before I could go home and collapse on the couch.

If you think back, there was always something driving you. When you were beat down, exhausted and ready to quit, your *WHY* was what kept you going. Thankfully, it was strong enough to pull you forward, and now you are a doctor!

Find Your "Why"

On your journey to financial independence, you must also have a *WHY* to guide you—and it should be compelling. It should be strong enough that you'll go through brick walls to get it. When you think about it, your stomach should flutter like it did when you met your first love. It should be your mind's last image before you sleep and your first thought when you wake up. It will drive you!

Determining your unique and personal *WHY* is the most important step in your journey to financial independence—and the first pillar that supports the pipeline to your future. Your path will be littered with obstacles and you will need something to drive you past them. Whatever vehicle you choose, your *WHY* is the fuel that powers it. Once you've filled your tank with *WHY*, your journey will have started!

Determining your unique and personal WHY is the most important step in your journey to financial independence—and the first pillar that supports the pipeline to your future.

My personal *WHY* was echoed a few years ago as I spoke to an orthopedic surgeon in Florida. We were having a great conversation when, suddenly, he said something that shocked me: "I hate vacations. They cost me money. Every time I go on vacation, all I can think about is the fact that my expenses continue to accumulate while I'm gone, and I'm not there bringing in revenue. It ruins my trip every time." That affected me deeply, not just because he was so honest, but because I used to have the exact same feelings.

It was summer 1996, and my wife and our two young children and I were eating ice cream from a quaint shop in the heart of the village in Vail, Colorado. This was our first one-week vacation after officially starting my medical practice. I had done a year of sports medicine training in Vail, and we love the mountains in the summer, so it seemed a perfect choice. We left on Saturday and were going to return the next Sunday so we could stretch the trip to as many days as possible. I couldn't afford to be away from my medical practice for more than a week—or so I thought.

We were visiting our friends, Brad and Jennifer, who were also there on vacation with their three children. Brad was an attorney and what he was telling me was driving me crazy. He and his family had rented their condo for a month and were contemplating renting it for the entire summer the next year. I thought, *How was he going to stay away from work that long? How was he going to pay the bills? If I left my orthopedic surgery practice for a month, I'd go broke.*

Brad still worked while he was there, but everything was done on the computer, so he didn't have to be in his office. He was in one of the world's most beautiful settings, yet he could make money and had plenty of time to play with his kids. In my mind, Brad was rich.

You see, travel was my big *WHY* and I told my wife that I wanted to do something like Brad and make money from anywhere in the world. I had never been taught how, but I knew there had to be a way. Not only would I make it from faraway places, but one day I would make it without my active input! I didn't want to "hate" my vacations. I was determined not to let money or work rule my life. I wanted freedom, so I set about learning how to get it.

What is it that you want deeply enough that nothing will stop you from getting it? Maybe you're fed up and want to quit medicine. I hope you don't, but if that is your burning *WHY* then I want to help you get there. Maybe you just want to have more control over your life or would like to travel. You might want to have the freedom to find a cure for cancer or take up a new hobby? The reasons are endless and what is most important is which reason is *YOURS*.

▶ **ACTION ITEM** ◀

Write down the six things you value the most to help you determine your "WHY."

Your unique vision of a wealthy life will drive you to do the extra work now to reap the benefits in the future. Once the *WHY* is embedded in your subconscious, the *HOW* and *WHAT* will take care of themselves.

So, if you know *WHY* you want to be rich, you are halfway there. The next step is to determine what "rich" means to you and how to get there.

What is Rich?

Honestly, who doesn't want to be rich? On the one hand, many would admit that, when they were young, they wanted to grow up to be rich and famous. On the other, we sometimes hear that money won't solve all our troubles and we should be mindful of the more "important" things in life. I couldn't agree more. Money alone doesn't produce real wealth and happiness, although it can give you a head start. As the late comedian Joan Rivers once said, "People say that money is not the key to happiness, but I always figured if you have enough money, you can have a key made!"

So, if money's a fundamental component of becoming rich, how are we taught to get it?

As early as grade school, we're warned that only college graduates can be successful. Once we enter the workforce, we're continually encouraged to secure higher levels of education through online degrees and Executive MBA programs. While this produces trainloads of specialists and mid-level managers, it's not a sure path to wealth. If the length of your schooling determined your wealth, physicians, lawyers, and PhDs would dominate the Forbes 500. Instead, it's filled with people like Michael Dell, Mark Zuckerberg, and Bill Gates, who all dropped out of school.

We're told that a high paycheck is the path to success. Yes, there are CEOs out there with massive salaries. If that's an option for you, go for it, but the positions are limited. For the rest of us, will a sizeable income make us rich? It's possible, but not with the wrong mindset. Bigger pay often brings bigger bills. I know plenty of people with six-figure incomes and six-figure expenses! If being rich is about having high paychecks, then we wouldn't have thousands of physicians on Facebook groups asking how to make extra money.

Early in my career, I had a big paycheck and was able to live well on 30 percent of my income—but then I got cocky. Soon enough, I was living on practically 100 percent of my income. The process is insidious and it happens fast. A big paycheck can fool you into feeling that you're secure. I've known plenty of folks with high incomes who were one paycheck away from financial chaos.

I once knew a doctor who made $600,000 a year but couldn't find enough money to pay his income taxes. He figured the money would always be there, so he never planned for the future. He had no real financial education and only got paid when he worked. He was living paycheck to paycheck on an income that put him in the top 1 percent of earnings! He was a poor doctor with high income. A big salary isn't the answer to financial freedom if you don't know how to use it.

We are told to save our money. It's prudent, of course, to have some savings for emergencies, but your money market fund won't make you rich. Banks have been paying less than 1 percent interest for almost a decade now. Even the magic of compounding interest won't turn that money into life-sustaining wealth. In fact, if all you do is save money, you will lose financially because inflation will outpace your interest returns.

We are taught to eliminate debt and live frugally. It's a great place to start, particularly if you are financially under water, but cutting up your credit cards and living on beans will not make you rich. Maybe after 20 years of drip coffee instead of skinny mocha lattes, you can take a two-week vacation instead of just one.

The frugal path to wealth was popularized in 1996 by Thomas Stanley's book, *The Millionaire Next Door*. Unfortunately, with mountains of student debt and inflation-adjusted lower salaries, today's young people don't stand a chance of getting rich by following Stanley's common-sense advice. It may have worked then, but the numbers don't work now if you want freedom from financial pressure. True wealth isn't created by living within your means; it's produced by expanding your means.

Of course, we're encouraged to "invest" in the stock market. Watching ticker tapes like a horse race has become a national pastime. It's up! It's down! Yes, some folks do well in the stock market, but the biggest windfalls are mostly enjoyed by those who sell those products, not the rank-and-file who bought them.

True wealth isn't created by living within your means; it's produced by expanding your means.

We are also taught to work more if we want more money. That's an option, but where does it stop? Can you work more than 24 hours a day? What would your life be like? "All work and no play" is tiresome and no way to live a happy, fulfilling life. Also, what happens when you stop working, by choice or by necessity? The money flow stops.

What's *your* definition of rich? Is it sitting on a big pile of money or getting paid top dollar for your services? Is it owning expensive cars, a big house, or a vacation home on the lake? Maybe it's having an extensive stock portfolio managed by a blue-chip financial advisor? Or, is it being free of student debt, working when you want to, not working, sleeping until noon, exploring new hobbies, traveling, or going to sleep at night knowing that you and your family are financially secure whether you work or not? There are many definitions of what makes one feel wealthy, but what does it take to achieve true financial freedom?

Defining True Wealth

In his book, *The Millionaire Real Estate Investor*, my friend Gary Keller writes about the difference between financial riches and financial wealth. He states that being rich is about having money. If you have a job that produces a lot of money, you might be rich. However, if you lose that job, you no longer have income and the cash dries up.

Financial wealth, on the other hand, is about owning assets that produce money whether you work or not. (Throughout the rest of the book, I will use the terms rich and wealth synonymously with the assumption that you are rich if you have income-producing assets.) Keller's words ring true and they define the theme that will pervade this book, which is to create financial freedom through passive income.

While the term "financial freedom" sounds like a hook from a self-help book or a weekend seminar, if you search your true feelings, it's what most of us are really after. Don't we look forward to the "freedom" of retirement when we no longer have to work? Isn't vacation a little taste of financial freedom?

If you have enough money to cover your expenses and your leisure activities with some leftover, you have some freedom. But if that money is derived from a job or an activity under someone else's control, you aren't truly free. To attain true financial independence, you must have income that comes from something you have reasonable control over.

Financial freedom means you can stop working today and still pay all your expenses. You either have a large bucket of money that won't run out before you die, or you've developed sufficient passive income to pay your expenses and support your lifestyle. Financial freedom means that money works for you. You're not truly free if you work for money.

This is a difficult paradigm shift for many people. We're brainwashed into thinking the only path is to work for most of our life and "invest" in the stock market to create a large bucket of money for retirement. How big does it need to be? I guess if you want to live a below-average retirement, you only need a small bucket. I presume those with a big bucket are considered rich. Are they really? Who's to say? What if that bucket of money runs out before you do? There are other paths to financial freedom and my mission is to introduce them to you.

Financial freedom means you can stop working today and still pay all your expenses.

Bestselling author Robert Kiyosaki often states that a simple definition of wealth is how many days you can survive without working. This may be simple, but it's brilliant. It doesn't put a number on wealth. It allows for an individualistic interpretation of wealth but provides a clear and finite understanding of what it looks like and, for some, a better idea of how to reach it.

Inner and Outer Wealth

Money doesn't make you rich.

For that, you need assets. As you'll learn in the following chapters, the right assets produce passive cash flow, which creates the time and freedom to better control your life. But to acquire true riches, you must change more than your bank account.

Every successful person I've met on my journey has had more than just money. There was a point when they determined the path to success and fulfillment involved a certain degree of personal development. These were wealthy, content, financially free people, but their lives were not without stress. However, they didn't identify the quality of their character by their bank balance. They were, above all, human beings, imperfect like all of us, but always striving to be better versions of themselves.

What I learned from them is while money and time might define financial freedom, they don't make up the full package. The attainment of money and time will make you appear wealthy to outsiders, and it might even fool you into thinking you've made it, but riches are empty if they don't enrich your life and the lives of those you touch.

This expanded idea of true fulfillment is addressed by Chris Martenson and Adam Taggart in their book, *Prosper!* It describes what they call the "eight forms of capital" that provide resilience and allow humans to coexist. They are listed below and can help you understand that real wealth goes beyond money and physical treasures. Each one plays a part in your journey to wealth and happiness while providing resilience against life's challenges.

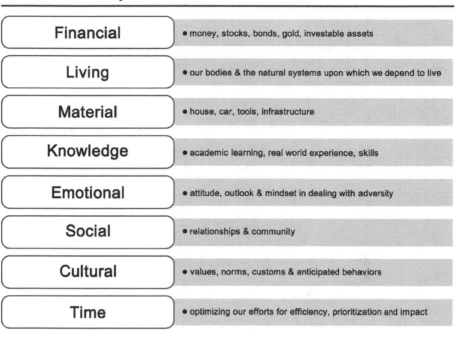

Forms of Capital	Definitions
Financial	• money, stocks, bonds, gold, investable assets
Living	• our bodies & the natural systems upon which we depend to live
Material	• house, car, tools, infrastructure
Knowledge	• academic learning, real world experience, skills
Emotional	• attitude, outlook & mindset in dealing with adversity
Social	• relationships & community
Cultural	• values, norms, customs & anticipated behaviors
Time	• optimizing our efforts for efficiency, prioritization and impact

Courtesy of PeakProsperity.com

The happiest and wealthiest people I've ever met dive deeply into these eight forms of capital. While they have money and time, they are also generous, friendly, smart, and worldly. They cultivate deep, meaningful relationships and contribute vast resources to the world. Money has simply magnified who they already were. In fact, I would argue that those qualities probably served them on their path to success.

Are Doctors Rich?

If you measure wealth by income, some doctors are rich. If you measure their wealth using the parameters described above, many will fall short. In fact, most highly paid professionals wouldn't fulfill our definition of rich.

Physicians enjoy a relatively high pay scale, and, based on national statistics, we're paid very well, even though income has dropped over the past 20 years. According to Glassdoor, physicians still hold the highest paying job in America.[4] Despite this enviable position, some never seem to get ahead. Often, they fall prey to Parkinson's Law, which, paraphrased, states that "expenses will rise to meet income."

This means that the more money we make, the more we tend to spend, creating an increase in consumption, which then requires ongoing expenditures to maintain that lifestyle. This is the raw material that forms the "golden handcuffs" of the highly paid physician, giving doctors a false sense of wealth and security early in their career. Only later do they start to feel trapped.

Let's compare Dr. Smith and John Doe. Dr. Smith is a surgeon and makes $400,000 a year with $400,000 of annual expenses. He leaves the house at 6 a.m. every morning and, after fighting with insurance companies, updating electronic medical records, and trying to compassionately care for his patients, returns home at 7 p.m., dead tired. He barely has time to say hello to his wife or remember his kids' names. He'll watch an hour of TV and then fall in bed so he can be ready for another day of life as a doctor. He knows if he doesn't get up the next morning, he'll make no money. In fact, he will lose money because he has an office full of employees that need to be paid twice a month.

John works five days a week, makes $50,000 a year and has $40,000 a year in expenses. Five years ago, John started investing in real estate. He plowed his meager savings into each project and worked weekends until eventually, he created a yearly cash flow of $40,000 in addition to his salary. His real estate properties now run without his effort and the checks show up every month.

When we compare these two, who is richer? Likely Dr. Smith lives in a nicer house, eats in better restaurants, and has a larger bank account. What does John Doe have? *He has time.* While his bank account remains small, he has repurchased the most precious asset on the planet.

John is now the master of his own time and can live his life without the need for a job. What he does with that time is his choice to make. His money is now working *for* him, and it works 24/7. If he's content, he can enjoy whatever passions his situation will allow. If he isn't, he now has the time to take on new projects. He can grow his real estate business to increase his income, or he can learn how to play the guitar. Either way, he has the time and the freedom to choose.

Working for money doesn't make you rich. No matter what your rate of pay, if you have to work to make your money, you are simply a highly paid poor person. As soon as you are unable to work, your income stops. Using that definition, most doctors, sadly, aren't rich.

No matter what your rate of pay, if you have to work to make your money, you are simply a highly paid poor person.

Wealth is a State of Mind

Henry David Thoreau said, "Wealth is the ability to fully experience life." What about you? Are you fully experiencing life? When you were a child, did you tell your parents you wanted to be a doctor because you wanted to work on a computer and input data into an electronic medical records system? Did you tell them you wanted to see more patients and spend less time with them so you could make your clinic manager proud of you and pay off your student debt? Not likely. You probably described healing the sick and helping those in need. You wanted to wear a white coat and save lives!

Is your goal to be the busiest doctor in town or to provide a good life for you and your family? If you're happy and content with your lifestyle, your work, your family, and your relationships, then you are already wealthy. If you are unsettled and unhappy or feel something is missing, you likely haven't yet attained the wealth and happiness you dreamed of when you were younger.

Wealth is a state of mind and the freedom to make choices without financial constraints. The next chapter is about cultivating a new attitude toward wealth, but first take a moment to consider this: What would it be like to never miss your kids sporting events, to cook breakfast for your children every morning, to take care of your grandkids while your children worked, or to travel as far as you want and as long as you want without worrying about missing patients or having to pay the rent? Consider what it would be like to practice medicine because you love it, not because you need it for the income. Think of the good you could do for society.

---

*Wealth is a state of mind and the freedom to make choices
without financial constraints.*

That's the wealth that I'm referring to in this book. I'm convinced you could make $1 million a year and be unhappy. Wealth isn't money. It is freedom, control and choices. Wealth is happiness and healthy relationships. It's giving and learning new things.

Now that you have a handle on why you want to be rich and you have a working definition of what *you* think is rich, turn the page and find out how the truly rich think!

BUILDING YOUR
PASSIVE INCOME PIPELINE

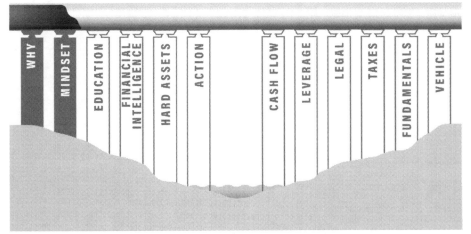

Chapter 4

Develop a Rich Mindset

For a man to conquer himself is the first and noblest of all victories.

—Plato

Why don't doctors get rich? Because most of them will skip this chapter.

Let's face it. There's a lot to keep track of out there and information bombards us from all directions. We are in a period of data overload that arrives in person, on the phone, by text and email, through professional journals, and on television—not to mention the terabytes of information pounding you daily from social media. Who has time to digest new material and try to change a thought process?

Like it or not, this torrent of information is shaping the way you think and affecting the results you are getting in your life.

The Power of Thought

Thoughts are powerful; they govern actions. Spiritual leader Mahatma Gandhi said this: "Your beliefs become your thoughts. Your thoughts become your words. Your words become your actions. Your actions become your habits. Your habits become your values. Your values become your destiny."

Your life is a mirror of your thoughts, so if you want to change your situation, you can't do it with the same thoughts that got you to where you are today. If you are searching for more joy and meaning in your life, you must start thinking like a "rich doctor."

This doesn't mean you should abandon your roots as a trained professional. It merely means that there is still untapped potential inside you that needs to be drawn out. Much of that potential has been overwhelmed by the intense education it took to become a doctor. Fortunately, it's still in there, and you can continue to be a great physician while unwrapping the rest of the package.

Your life is a mirror of your thoughts, so if you want to change your situation, you can't do it with the same thoughts that got you to where you are today.

Some of you may be thinking right about now, "Just get to the numbers, Tom. I don't need all this self-help talk." That's exactly what I said over 25 years ago. I was a slow and resistant student. Had I been more open-minded, I might have succeeded even faster. We'll get to the details of financial success soon enough, but it's of paramount importance to understand that you will never manifest true riches unless you are open to thinking about money, relationships, and personal development as part of the same journey.

Wealth begins with mindset. In fact, "thought process" is so vital that author and speaker Brian Tracy coined a term called "The Law of Attraction." This describes the curious fact that you will attract what you think about the most. People and resources that help bring your thoughts to life will almost magically appear. You thought about being a doctor for years, now here you are! What are the possibilities if you think about being rich?

So, how do wealthy people think?

Money Is Only a Tool

Let's get this elephant off our back right at the beginning. How do you think about money? Would you do anything for money, or have you been taught that money corrupts? Money is neither righteous nor evil. It's simply a medium of exchange for obtaining goods and services. The love of money itself, without consideration for what good it can do, is the problem. The wealth you accumulate can be put into service to do good or harm. The choice is yours.

In the Charles Dickens classic, *A Christmas Carol*, the main character, Ebenezer Scrooge, was a lonely, friendless old man whose only love was money. He sought and loved his precious gold coins and shared them with no one. Over the course of one night, three spirits— the ghosts of Christmas Past, Present, and Future—showed him the good that his money could do versus the folly of his greed, and what would happen if he didn't change his ways. Scrooge's eyes were opened, and rather than die friendless and desolate, he decided to share his wealth and lived out his remaining days loved and admired, by enriching the lives of others.

Money doesn't change people; it just magnifies who we really are. Scrooge was a miser from the beginning. When he became the richest man in town, he was also the biggest miser. When he discovered generosity, he was the most generous man in town. So, it stands to reason that we would want to become the best version of ourselves, knowing that wealth will magnify who we really are.

Make money your servant and not your master.

To some, money is a yardstick for measuring their success. Those are simply poor people with big bank accounts. To the genuinely wealthy, money is a tool and can be a servant that works for them 24 hours a day without complaint. It can be used to serve others and is a natural reward for improving our world in some way. Make money your servant and not your master.

Rein in Your Ego

Physicians spend a lot of their lives training. There are difficult classes, grueling tests, and brutal selection processes. After surviving all that, most doctors are proud of their accomplishments, and they should be. There are 328 million people in the United States as of 2019, and about a million of those are physicians.[5, 6] That means only 0.3 percent of the population can do what we do, putting doctors in elite company. It also means that over 99 percent of the population likely can do something we can't. This fact is sometimes lost on physicians, whose great skill in one area does not always translate well into others.

I learned this lesson the hard way during the early stages of my real estate investing career. I found a private opportunity I wanted to invest in. I had learned to seek advice from a knowledgeable third party, so I did just that, taking it to a close friend who had years of real estate experience. His opinion was that the deal favored the sponsor and not the investors. Up until then, I had followed good advice. But this time, greed and ego got in the way and I ignored his counsel. It "felt" like a good deal to me, so I invested. Within 18 months, everything my friend predicted happened. I lost money but learned a valuable lesson: I didn't know everything.

Yes, physicians are usually bright. They must be to survive the training and selection process and receive their credentials. However, here's a newsflash: A medical degree does not convey omnipotence and knowledge about all things in life. I've met some doctors who believe that because they've been so smart in the medical world, they automatically know business, real estate, investing, and law. This reminds me of a doctor joke that goes like this: "What's the difference between God and a doctor? Answer: God doesn't think he is a doctor!"

I once spoke to a pharmaceutical representative who related this story: "I had a friend who became an orthopedic surgeon. I became a salesman and worked for a pharmaceutical company. As fate would have it, he was in my territory and I visited him often. One day, I brought lunch to his office to introduce a new drug that I felt would be useful for his patients. I had been there many times and we had a great relationship. That day, he stopped me and said, 'You drug reps waste my time. What could you possibly tell me that I don't already know?'"

Having been in sales, I had experienced the same type of customer. I asked the salesman how he responded. He said that he didn't press the issue because he knew his friend wouldn't be receptive. As we talked, he shared other such encounters with physicians in the past. He said that while he understood their level of education, he felt sorry for them because their arrogance or lack of curiosity was keeping them from learning things that could improve their lives and their patients' health.

We all have egos, but to succeed in life, and especially if you want to become financially free, you must leave ego out of your decision-making. Ego gets attached to what we've accomplished in the past and can blind us from seeing what we can achieve in the future.

In his book *Ego is the Enemy*, Ryan Holiday quotes the ancient Greek Stoic philosopher Epictetus, who said, "It is impossible to learn that which one thinks one already knows." As Holiday paraphrases, "You can't get better if you already think you're the best."

Cultivate Humility

The opposite of ego is humility. Humility isn't a deficiency. It can be an ally and a powerful tool as you work with others to create your personal financial freedom. Humility allows you to build relationships that could enrich your life and your bank account. It keeps your eyes open for new opportunities and enables you to ask questions to learn and grow.

Some of the wealthiest people in the world are known to be quite humble, including Mark Zuckerberg of Facebook, Berkshire Hathaway's Warren Buffett, and Apple's CEO, Tim Cook. Great world leaders such as Abraham Lincoln, George Washington, and Benjamin Franklin were famously humble folks.

Humility also allows for proper teamwork, and teams are critical to long-term financial success. Teams will be discussed in later chapters, but the main takeaway is that if you can't "play with others," you won't be able to function on a team. That will limit your potential.

Have a Positive Attitude

Victor Frankel, Holocaust survivor, neurologist, and author of *Man's Search for Meaning*, once said, "Everything can be taken from a man but one thing: the last of the human freedoms—to choose one's attitude in any given set of circumstances, to choose one's own way." His choice of attitude was crucial in his survival of the Auschwitz concentration camp in Nazi-occupied Poland during World War II.

Attitude also plays a pivotal role in success and wealth. Often, it's more important than experience or ability. The right attitude exhibits "possibility thinking" as opposed to cynicism and skepticism. Our emotions are determined primarily by how we interpret events.

I've had pragmatic professionals tell me that no matter how I think about it, a problem will not miraculously go away if I simply "think positive." I totally agree. Positive thinking won't cure an infection, make you a scratch golfer, or fill an empty bank account—and that's the point. Whatever the issue, you are going to have to roll up your sleeves and fix it.

The choice you have is whether to see it as an opportunity or a roadblock. Either way, it's still there, but if you approach the challenge with a positive attitude, it will become a valuable teacher, rather than a waste of time and resources. The decision is ours; we have total control over how we interpret any situation.

Attitude is determined by how you interpret the events around you, not by the events themselves.

There's a story that goes like this: Many years ago, two salesmen were sent by a British shoe manufacturer to Africa to investigate its market potential. The first salesman returned disappointed, and with a defeated attitude reported, "There is no potential here—nobody wears shoes." The second salesman burst into the boardroom, overflowing with excitement and exclaimed, "There is massive potential here—nobody has shoes!" It's all about attitude.

To put this into a modern context, if a surgery case gets delayed, or a client doesn't show up, you can choose how to react. You can complain about the situation, or you can look at it as an opportunity to get other work done, catch up on your reading, or call to check in on a family member. Either way, the situation isn't going to change.

According to Mark Victor Hansen, author of *Chicken Soup for the Soul*, "It's your state of mind, not your circumstances, that determines whether it will be a good day or a bad day." Attitude is determined by how you interpret the events around you, not by the events themselves. If the choice is to be upset and angry versus relieved to have some free time, choose the latter.

Attitude will also influence who you attract to your mission. Would you rather work with positive thinkers who regularly hurdle obstacles or negative thinkers who can't see past the problems? Keep a positive and resilient attitude. You'll get rich faster and the ride will be a lot more fun.

Mind Your Words

A major component of a positive attitude is the words we use. As noted at the beginning of this chapter, words are powerful and can define our actions. If we are to produce a wealthy mindset and hence, a wealthy life, we should reinforce it by using the right words. And that will start with your beliefs.

Your subconscious mind filters your words to fit into a pattern that's consistent with your inner beliefs. For example, if you feel you aren't talented or worthy enough to reach a lofty goal, you might respond to a challenge by saying, "I could never do that," and your reality will reinforce that belief! But it also works in the other direction, and how will you know unless you try? So set yourself up for success by using your words accordingly.

The chart below highlights some examples of rich doctor words and poor doctor words. Many of these concepts will be covered in future chapters.

Poor Doctor Words	Rich Doctor Words
I don't have time	I prioritize my time
It's too risky	I manage risk with knowledge
I'm not paid enough	I create my own income
Professionals handle my money	I control my own investments
That won't work here	I will learn how to make it work
I have a high salary	I have freedom
I have status	I have cash flow
Many people work for me	I serve many people
I have years of higher education	I am a continuous learner

Try this experiment. As you speak to people, pay attention to the words you use. Are they rich doctor words or poor doctor words?

Develop Discipline and Good Habits

Discipline is a key factor in reaching most goals, including financial freedom. Anyone who has completed professional schooling or received an advanced degree has typically exhibited true discipline to reach that level of success. If that mindset can be carried forward in the pursuit of wealth, it will serve you well.

Discipline is born out of habits. We've all developed habits. Some are good and some are not so good. It's a funny thing, but it seems a lot easier to develop bad routines than good ones. I may never understand that aspect of human nature, except for the fact that we are pleasure-seeking creatures and certain inclinations offer a quick way there.

It takes an average of 66 days to form a habit—less for some folks, more for others.[7] However long it takes, you can turn a new activity into a process that your brain will perceive as normal and necessary. That's a small price to pay for something that will enrich you for the rest of your life.

Wealthy people create good habits. Constructive practices, combined with the discipline to persevere, are necessary ingredients for success. The happiest, wealthiest folks I've met usually have a small number of deeply ingrained, wealth-producing patterns they follow each day. Most are small and seem insignificant but have lasting, cumulative, positive effects. The most common ones include a commitment to personal development, life-long education, honesty, meditation, focus, early rising, and delegation.

It takes discipline to create a productive habit, but once established, that new mode of operation helps you to move forward when life places roadblocks in your path. For doctors, it takes a strong dose of discipline to break away from the education that prepared you for your profession but didn't teach you to be rich.

To create wealth, you would be well-advised to develop the habits of the wealthy. According to Brian Tracy, "Successful people are simply those with successful habits." (For a free download containing more detail on the habits of success, go to www.richdoctor.com/tools)

Set Goals

Hopefully, it's becoming evident that wealth has a lot to do with how you think—not just numbers and bank balances. You must be driven by something to become wealthy, something that inexorably *pulls* you toward success: a goal that will change your life in a way that will make you happy. Goals have a unique way of getting us through adversity. If you have a concrete idea of what you really want, you will find a way to get it.

Think back to medical school, law school, or college. What was your goal then? To pull all-nighters, take tests, and occasionally get humiliated by teachers and mentors? No. The goal was to become a doctor, lawyer, or college graduate. That gave you the fortitude to fight on and endure any hardships to get what you wanted. That's the power of a goal.

One of my most poignant goal setting lessons came from my son when he was in high school. He was a wrestler. He loved it and he was good at it. He would rise before 6 a.m. every morning and train with his best friend before class, then he would practice after school. For those of you who don't know wrestling, it's a grueling sport, pitting you against the other guy, *mano a mano*. If you lose, there is no one to blame. The training is tough, and many drop out.

Before his junior season began, he boldly proclaimed that he would win the state title. Some would call this a "big, hairy, audacious goal" (BHAG). It was pretty audacious because there was no indication that he was remotely good enough to do that. Up to that point, I was just proud that he had the mental strength to stick with the sport.

He worked hard all year, surprisingly losing only one match to the top-ranked wrestler in the state of Texas. This was early in the season, and after the match, the opposing coach and wrestler were blatantly dismissive when he went over to them for the customary congratulatory handshake. This affected him deeply. His primary goal was to win state, but now he just wanted another shot at that opponent.

During that year, he developed a habit of working hard every day, never wavering from his training. As we neared the state tournament, he was ranked #2 and the wrestler who had handed him his only defeat was ranked #1. My son had been abnormally tired the entire school year, but he figured it was just nerves. (Later we found out he had mononucleosis.) He never broke training and never lost focus.

Poetically, the two met in the finals. It was an epic match. With eight seconds left, my son was down by a point and in a bad position, looking very much like he was headed to another second-place finish. Suddenly, he manufactured a move that gave him two points. The buzzer sounded and he was state champion!

When he was interviewed later and asked what he was thinking at that moment, he replied, "Keep wrestling. I was taught to fight until the whistle blows."

My son never quit because he had a goal to reach and he refused to let anything get in the way, including an infection that would put most people in bed. Now, when things get tough in medicine or business, his example of dedication and perseverance gives me the strength to keep fighting.

Your personal growth is the true magic of a belief-stretching goal.

To achieve your dreams, you must fight until the whistle blows. Because on the road to financial freedom, you will always be tested by roadblocks, disappointments, and disasters.

What supported my son, and what will carry you through those tough moments, is an ultimate goal. Your journey to wealth begins with a vision of your future, an objective that truly excites you. This vision will define your progress and help you endure inevitable hardships. The more "big, hairy and audacious" the goal, the better!

A goal should be more than a target to aim at. It should be big enough that it stretches your capabilities and inner beliefs. That's how you grow and that's how you will achieve things that you previously thought were impossible.

The true purpose of a goal is not necessarily to reach it, but to become the person you need to be to reach that goal. Your personal growth is the true magic of a belief-stretching goal. As you strive to reach your highest objective, the more likely you will find your true purpose in life and perhaps have a profound effect on the world around you.

Finally, write down your goals. Sit down and list 100 things you would like to accomplish in life. It will take time, but it will give you guidance and insight into what is most important to you. Review them at regular intervals. Remember, nothing is too big or too audacious, and the sky is the limit. There is no ceiling on your personal dreams and desires.

> ▶ **ACTION ITEM** ◀
> Write down 100 goals you would like to achieve
> in your lifetime.

Create Focus

Goals create focus. John Maxwell writes that successful people have learned to focus 80 percent of their effort on the 20 percent of activities that produce the best results. As it turns out, that is a reproducible ratio. In 1906, Italian economist Vilfredo Pareto observed that 80 percent of the land in Italy was owned by 20 percent of the people.[8]

This observation was later generalized by others in the field of economics and is now known as the Pareto Principle or the 80/20 rule. It states that 80 percent of the consequences come from 20 percent of the causes.[9] Thus, if you want to solve 80 percent of your problems, you only have to focus on the most important 20 percent of your life. Focus is efficient and rich doctors like to be efficient.

One of the best and most practical books I've read on focus is *The New York Times* bestseller, *The One Thing*, written by Gary Keller and Jay Papasan. Not only does it discuss wealth principles; it encourages you to identify *the one thing you can do today* to help you reach your goals.

The most memorable metaphor in the book is "the domino effect." Once you start the reaction, a single domino can knock over a second domino that is 50 percent greater in size. If you carry that forward, eventually you can knock over a domino of almost unlimited size. Likewise, if you focus on achieving the most important thing now and carry that victory forward, eventually you can have almost unlimited success!

Develop Persistence

Creating a focused plan is, in some ways, the easy part. The hard part is keeping on track because life will try to derail you. As boxer Mike Tyson famously said, "Everybody has a plan until they get punched in the face." If you want to achieve your goals, you can't quit when the going gets tough. You must develop persistence.

If you have crystallized your goals, developed good habits, and cultivated discipline, you are that many steps closer to success and financial freedom. But even with that, your road to financial freedom will not be a straight line. If it's anything like mine, you will have detours, dead ends, and many crashes!

Your most valuable asset may be your willingness to persist longer than anyone else.

I have gone down so many rabbit holes I should have grown a fuzzy tail by now. Each time I hit a dead end, all I could think of was my old football coach yelling at me to keep my head down, my knees high, and to keep running! It was his way of telling me to focus on the process and not to quit. That blind faith gave me enough energy to finish the play. As an adult, it gave me the will to move past the failures and on to the next challenge, ultimately leading to success.

Life is going to punch you in the face, probably more than once. As long as you keep getting up, your chances of success increase. Your most valuable asset may be your willingness to persist longer than anyone else.

Always Be Growing

I've been a reader my entire life. I prefer spy novels, real estate books, and sports biographies. At one stage in my life, I joined the Amway organization. Network marketing made sense to me and I figured that, at the least, I would learn to sell. What I didn't realize is that they had a huge personal development program with books, tapes, and seminars. It was during this time that I discovered many of the classics in the personal development world.

For years, my wife has jokingly called these my "you can do it" books, but I still love reading them. A few of the classics included *Think and Grow Rich* by Napolean Hill, *The Seven Habits of Highly Effective People* by Stephen Covey, and *The Magic of Thinking Big* by David Schwartz. These were refreshingly different from the medical journals I read to keep up with my profession.

As I learned more and started associating with successful people, I found that they were reading many of the same books that I was! It was during this time that I discovered how important our "thought process"—the way we think—is if we want to achieve success. I read everything I could get my hands on and made it a point to associate with folks who were moving forward. I needed a lot of help! I discovered that truly successful people were focused yet open-minded. They double-checked the numbers and yet were perpetually optimistic. They didn't follow the crowd but worked well with teams. They were grateful for what they had and were generous.

To be truly rich on the outside, you must also become wealthy on the inside.

I've also come to realize that true success is a continuous journey. Personal development is like golf. The bad news is that you're never as good as you want to be. The good news is that, if you want to improve your game, you've always got something to look forward to!

There is an anonymous quote that states, "The definition of hell is that on your last day on earth, the person you became will meet the person you could have become." We all have great potential, but not everyone chooses to nurture that potential. To be truly rich on the outside, you must also become wealthy on the inside.

I really didn't develop true freedom until I discovered more about who I am and how I needed to grow personally. This, coupled with a relatively sound plan for passive cash flow to replace my expenses, has given me a comfortable life. I want the same for you. That's why I'm writing this book—so you can take advantage of what I learned the hard way and succeed faster than I did.

BUILDING YOUR

PASSIVE INCOME PIPELINE

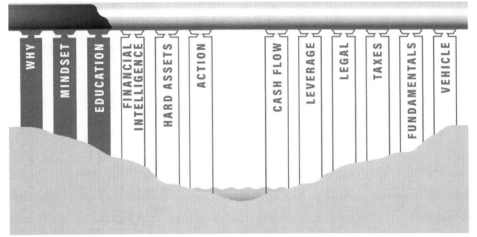

YOUR
NOW

YOUR
FUTURE

WHY · MINDSET · EDUCATION · FINANCIAL INTELLIGENCE · HARD ASSETS · ACTION · CASH FLOW · LEVERAGE · LEGAL · TAXES · FUNDAMENTALS · VEHICLE

Chapter 5

Get a Rich Education

Formal education will make you a living; self-education will make you a fortune.

—JIM ROHN

In 1978, the movie *Animal House* was released. While this low-budget film was largely unknown at the time and most of its stars were just starting their careers, 40 years later it's considered one of the greatest comedies ever made.

A satire of the fraternity and sorority scene in the early 60's, the movie centers around the prestigious Omega Theta Pi fraternity and the outcasts of Delta Tau Chi. It takes place at the fictitious Faber College, founded by Emil Faber. At one point in the movie, the camera is following some important characters when it pans past a statue of Faber in the center of campus. Carved into the base of the statue are the sage words of the college's fictitious founder: "Knowledge is good."

While that may be comically unprofound T-shirt material, no one would argue with Emil Faber. Knowledge *is* good, but our success depends on what knowledge we seek, who we get it from, and what we do with it. Doctors, for example, have plenty of knowledge. So why aren't they all rich? The answer is that they were taught to heal, not to be rich. Our system wasn't designed for that.

Traditional Education vs. Wealth Education

In 1902, the General Education Board (GEB) was founded by John D. Rockefeller, Sr., and Frederick Gates to promote education throughout the United States.[10] In 1904, the Board issued a report on the school system. The purpose of the report, according to G. Edward Griffin, author of *The Creature from Jekyll Island*, "…was not to raise the level of education, but to influence the direction of that education."

Griffin goes on to say that, "The object was to use the classroom to teach attitudes that encourage people to be passive and submissive to their rulers. The goal was—and is—to create citizens who are educated enough for productive work under supervision but not enough to question authority or seek to rise above their class."[11]

Later, in their very first publication, the GEB stated, "In our dreams we have limitless resources, and the people yield themselves with perfect docility to our molding hands."[12]

Do you want to be molded, or do you want to prosper?

We have one of the finest educational systems in the world and it produces great doctors, lawyers, and accountants. However, if you speak to anyone who has been through the system, he or she will tell you that they were never taught about money. I recently spoke with a lawyer who lamented that his peers know how to make money, but they don't know how to run a business. One of the best-known CPAs in the country once told me he was taught to count money and do taxes but not how to become wealthy or to have money work for him. Sadly, the caricature of a physician is similar: someone who can make money but doesn't know what to do with it.

Who is going to teach us? Most of our schooling is provided by teachers who use theory as the basis of their instruction. There are real advantages to this approach: It allows for someone who isn't Einstein to give us lessons on math and for someone who wasn't physically at the Battle of Waterloo to explain history. However, when it comes to advising on how to be rich, experience counts. Sadly, though they perform an immeasurable service to society, most teachers don't have the track record to teach wealth formation.

If you want the blueprint on how to be rich, you must get the it from people who have already built their wealth.

Our educational system is rigid, designed to teach the masses how to function and survive in modern society. It was also intended to produce highly trained specialists, such as physicians. There's no question that it makes us good doctors. But the system lacks financial education, which limits our options to become "rich doctors."

I would be hypocritical if I didn't acknowledge that I grew up in the traditional system and thrived in it. By the time I was 30, I could fix the most disastrously injured knee you can imagine, but I knew nothing about the world of the rich. The traditional system wasn't going to take me there, so I needed a better option. I needed wealth education!

Emil Faber was right. Knowledge is good, and education is a vital component in the production of wealth. But your personal success depends on what you want to learn and where you get your information. If you want the blueprint on how to be rich, you must get the it from people who have already built their wealth. The good news is that wisdom is more available to you than ever before. You just have to look for it.

Become a Reader

It was February 1999 and I was in Inawashiro, Japan, as the physician for the U.S. Olympic Freestyle Ski Team. My job was to keep these 16 to 24-year-old athletes healthy so they could compete. One day, as we were moving from one venue to another, I noticed something very strange. As we settled into our seats on the bus, it seemed like every other athlete pulled out the same book and began reading. I asked if it was some sort of group study and they said no, it was a new book about wizards and witches called *Harry Potter and the Sorcerer's Stone*.

My own backpack contained Dale Carnegie's classic, *How to Win Friends and Influence People*, *Multiple Streams of Income*, and a book about leadership. While I eventually figured out who Harry Potter was, I realized that my focus was on something different than entertainment. I was on a personal mission to become rich and slowly learning that to do so—to do something I had never done before—I had to change my thought process. The simplest and easiest place to start that education was to begin reading books written by people who had already accomplished what I wanted to do.

> **▶ ACTION ITEM ◀**
> Commit to reading at least a few pages of a success-oriented book every day.

When I made the commitment to focus on my financial education, I read everything under the sun. For me they were mostly about real estate, which I chose as my path to wealth. Some books had a tremendous impact while others provided ideas that I tucked away for later use.

Find books written by the people who are doing what you want to do. No matter your interest, there's enough information out there to keep you busy for the rest of your life, and you will still have more to learn. Today, with the click of a button, you can have the advice of an expert on your computer immediately, or at your door within hours. A $15.95 book might just change your life! It changed mine.

Remember the story of the car wash? To put things in perspective, it set me back $19.95 to get my truck washed, and that only lasted a week. The $15.95 I invested in *Rich Dad Poor Dad* accelerated my path to lifelong financial freedom. So, I ask you, if you get just one idea from a book, is it worth the price?

My purchase of a single book in 1997 started a 20-year friendship with Robert Kiyosaki, who is a worldwide celebrity in the world of personal finance. The education, mentorship, and inspiration I've received from that relationship have had a priceless influence on the success I've achieved. It all started with a drive to continually educate myself and the willingness to read an obscure book, by an unknown author, sold at a car wash. (For a list of book titles to help you get started, go to www.richdoctor.com/tools)

A $15.95 book might just change your life!

Attend Seminars

I soon discovered through personal experience that while reading was a great start, I needed a deeper level of learning if I was to achieve financial freedom. So I started looking for teachers with experience. My first contact was with one of those free seminars given by a financial services firm to doctors. This was obviously a marketing function for the company, but I learned enough at that two-hour presentation to encourage me to look further.

Over the next 30 years, I attended seminars on a myriad of topics including general investing, stock trading, mobile homes, discount notes, asset protection, syndication, goalsetting, speaking, teaching, and sales. The actual list is too long to reproduce.

These seminars were always taught by people who had already succeeded in the subject they were teaching. They weren't using theories learned in books and they hadn't typically obtained a PhD by pouring through research papers and developing a dissertation. They were in the trenches and had real-world experience to share with the students in the room. They talked about their successes—and their blunders. It was easy to pay attention!

Often, the seminar leader would use real-world situations to demonstrate the subject of the day. Typically, we would discuss this as a group after the session. The seminars that I found most useful were those where the leader would orchestrate simulations to help us learn in greater detail. Simulation is only one step removed from doing the real thing and for me, that led to a deeper understanding of the subject and greater retention of the information.

Learning is a continuum. It starts with reading and ends with actual experience. It is postulated that we remember 10 percent of what we read and up to 90 percent of what we say and do.[13] The closer we get to the real thing, the more we tend to absorb and internalize. While my reading was improving my knowledge base, the seminars were solidifying that education.

Think back to your own training. During the clinical portion of medical school, we were typically taught by physicians actively caring for patients in the real world every day. This was valuable education and similar to how other professions and trades are taught. Attorneys are trained by other attorneys. Plumbers serve an apprenticeship under an experienced plumber. New real estate agents learn under an experienced broker. Karate students learn under a master.

The passing on of first-hand knowledge by experts is a powerful way to get an education. So the question is this: Who is training you to be a wealth professional?

In my case, my passion eventually led me to real estate. Over the past 25 years, I've been trained by some of the most successful real estate entrepreneurs in the world. These people have been through the fires of building successful careers and they passed that wisdom on to me through seminars and courses. As I learned from their experiences, my knowledge deepened. I was able to avoid some of the mistakes they made, and I've tried to emulate the characteristics that made them successful.

Nothing replaces hands-on experience, but learning from those who have attained the success you desire is the next best thing—and that education is readily available.

Don't Fear Mistakes

Mistakes are bad, right?

That's what we've been taught. Anybody who has been through our school system has been trained to believe that the right answers are good and wrong answers are bad, something to be avoided at all costs. So why talk about mistakes in a chapter about education? Because mistakes often give us our greatest lessons.

For most of our conscious development, we are rewarded for being "right" and punished in some way for being "wrong." We get praise for a good report card. We get a star on our paper in first grade. We are given the title of valedictorian if we are the one person who was "most right" in high school or college. And to be fair, we do want our doctors, lawyers, and advisors to be right most of the time. But we are stigmatized for failure.

Throughout the course of your life and while you are building your wealth, you will make mistakes. I know there's an A-student out there who is mistake averse and now thinking about throwing this book in the trash. But if you hold on for just a minute, I will show you that mistakes are not only okay but are often the first step to something better!

Never waste a good mistake—embrace the lesson and succeed!

Thomas Edison is well-known for his work in perfecting the incandescent electric light bulb and other impressive feats of science. What is less well-known is that he worked tirelessly for months to develop a nickel-iron battery. At one point, his friend Walter S. Mallory found Edison sitting at a large table with hundreds of test batteries in front of him. Knowing Edison had tried over nine-thousand experiments without success, he said, "Isn't it a shame that with the tremendous amount of work you have done, you haven't been able to get any results?" To which Edison replied, "Results! Why, man, I've gotten a lot of results! I know several thousand things that won't work."[14]

Edison didn't perceive failures as negative events but rather as steps along the way to success. This perception gave him the ability to persist through each successive setback. Edison made dealing with failure look easy, but this is no simple achievement. Though you'd like to believe that you'll be levelheaded enough to recognize each of your failures as bringing you a step closer to success, that probably won't happen. I've had plenty of failures, and while I now see the value of those lessons, at the time I was not a happy camper.

I bought an apartment complex around 2000, before I had enough experience to do it correctly. It went bad and I barely escaped with my money. I've also blindly trusted people and paid the price when I discovered they were either incompetent or crooks. I have started restaurants that failed, sold lighters nationwide and made nothing, and invested in projects because I liked the sponsor but didn't check the numbers. All these events were failures, but they did not define me. They were simply experiences that taught me valuable lessons.

The people who have been the most successful in life and in business are those who have failed the most. This is hard to grasp at first, but a study of people who have done great things reveals that their victories were often preceded by defeat.

Walt Disney was fired from a newspaper because he "lacked imagination and had no good ideas," yet he founded an iconic company that embodies imagination. The first company Bill Gates and Paul Allen created failed, but they used the lessons learned to build Microsoft. These successful visionaries had the ability to use failure as a learning experience to create long-term success.

If you want to be rich, you will fail along the way—sorry, it happens but you'll get over it. Bad things are going to happen and you will deal with them. Mistakes are so much a part of the fabric of success that Ryan Holiday wrote a book about it called *The Obstacle is the Way*. His theory is that obstacles are not only common in life, but they are an integral part of true success. So never waste a good mistake––embrace the lesson and succeed!

Learn to Sell

This is where I may lose a few of you because doctors don't have to sell, right? Think again. As Robert Louis Stevenson said, "Everyone lives by selling something."

Physicians sell themselves daily. If they didn't, they wouldn't have any patients, which would produce no revenue. As soon as you walk through the exam room door, you are selling.

According to *Psychological Science*, it takes a mere one-tenth of a second to make a first impression.[15] Even the clothing you wear has a significant effect on how people categorize you going forward.[16] While you may not be conscious of it, you likely try to dress the part of a doctor. I doubt you would show up in the office in shorts and flip flops. That is selling.

Sales isn't about convincing someone that they need a product or a surgery; it's about influencing their thought process to help them get what they want.

You are kind and responsive to referring physicians so they will keep sending you patients. When you are at a party and someone asks what you do, you tell them you're a doctor and likely expand on your area of expertise. If my experience is any indication, many of the people you meet will ask for free advice, but some will ask for your card in case they need you in the future. That's sales and marketing.

All entrepreneurs must be able to sell. If you are starting a company, you will have to explain your vision to investors and customers and do so with enthusiasm and confidence. If you are raising money for an investment, you must describe the value it brings to investors. If you want to work with a mentor, you will need to convince him or her that you have a passion to learn.

Sales isn't about convincing someone that they need a product or a surgery; it's about influencing their thought process to help them get what *they* want. Patients want to be healthy and investors want to make money. With experience and education, you can help them achieve their goals. So embrace the fact that we all sell something and that it's an honorable way to help others. And the next time you have a sales rep in your office, be kind. They are there to help you and probably have a family to feed, just like you!

Grow Your Network

We spend more time with our medical colleagues than we do with our families. We are part of a medical "tribe" that molds our thoughts and shapes our paradigms. If we hang around doctors and nurses all day, we will view our circumstances through that filter. There is nothing wrong with that, but if you want to break out of your current routine and play a bigger game, you will need to find a new tribe that stretches your capabilities.

Motivational speaker Jim Rohn famously said, "We are the average of the five people we spend the most time with." Who are you spending time with, and are they helping you achieve your goals? Do they challenge you to succeed higher and faster?

Who you spend time with is who you will become. So it's important to surround yourself with positive people who are moving in the direction you want to go, and it is equally important to avoid negative people. Their attitudes, mindsets, and thought processes will become part of your own, so choose your network carefully.

> ► **ACTION ITEM** ◄
> List the five people you spend the most time with
> and determine if they are helping you grow and
> achieve your goals.

Through these relationships, you'll discover things you don't know and things you need to know to succeed in your mission. Take, for example, playing the guitar. If you hang around guitar players, you will absorb their culture and opportunities to learn and play will magically appear. If you want to create financial freedom, seek out people who are already there, or are trying to get there. Opportunities will find you. Once you start associating with people who are moving in a similar direction, you will organically develop the drive and inspiration to achieve your goal. It's a symbiotic relationship and is a multiplier that benefits all parties.

One thing to keep in mind is that a successful life is built on how much you serve others. Try to avoid categorizing people by what they can do for you. When you meet new people, think of how you can add value to *their* life or mission. When you're networking, don't walk into a room to see what you can *get*. Walk into a room to see what you can *give*.

This was emphasized by author and speaker, Zig Ziglar, who said, "You will have all you want in life, if you help enough other people get what they want." Your mindset in joining a network is to add value. With that goal in mind, you can't help but find success!

I know this sounds hokey, but you must believe that you can do it—that you can learn what you need to achieve your dream. If you believe you can only be a doctor with no time for anything else, you'll be right. If you believe that you can become financially free, you will create that reality. You begin by absorbing the knowledge of others and then continuing to educate yourself. The basic definition of education is to "develop skills or knowledge that you don't already have." You did that to become a doctor. Now do it to become a rich doctor!

PASSIVE INCOME PIPELINE

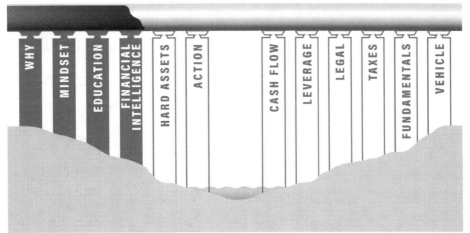

Chapter 6

Know the Rules of the Game

The Golden Rule: Whoever has the gold makes the rules.

— "Wizard of Id" comic strip, 1964

I magine that you are the most gifted athlete in the world and are asked to play in a World Cup soccer match. The catch is that you grew up in the jungles of the Amazon and you've never seen a soccer game in your life. You don't know the rules. The game starts and the first thing you do is tackle the opposing player, grab the ball with your hands, and run off the field. Not only does this create a penalty but it could get you mugged in some countries! How successful will you be as a player and a teammate if you don't know the rules?

That's the problem in the world of money. The rules of the game are not always evident, and sometimes they don't seem to be written for us. That doesn't have to be the case. As you learn the rules of money you will develop *financial intelligence*. A strong financial intelligence will give you the ability to see opportunity and to avoid calamity. It will allow you to make decisions more rapidly and with more certainty. This will be one of your advantages.

Armed with a robust financial intelligence, you'll have a better chance of being a winner and building a productive, durable pipeline. One set of rules made you a good doctor—mastering the rules of money will make you a rich doctor.

Who is Grading You?

When you were young, did your parents encourage you to study hard and get good grades so that you could get a good job? I know mine did. I still believe it's a good idea to study hard and get good grades, but in the real world, your success depends more on who's grading you and what they are grading you on.

In school we were given numerical grades which provided a system used to rank you in order of class "intelligence." This ranking system haunted you throughout your academic career and eventually formed the basis on which people compared you to others. I suspect some of you remember the anxiety of wondering if your grades were high enough to get you into medical school. Once you did get in, this ranking pattern continued, which affected your ability to get the residency training you desired.

To some of you, these were simply the rules of the game. To others, they were a constant source of angst. But those rules don't matter anymore.

If you want to be rich, leave that grading system in the past. In the world of the rich, you are graded on a different set of numbers. You will never be asked for your school transcript. Bankers, partners, and investors evaluate you based on your financial statement. A strong financial statement means that you've had a strong financial education.

The Financial Statement

The financial statement consists of an income statement and balance sheet. For those of you who've had some financial education or took a business class during your schooling, this might be review. For others, this is new territory so pay close attention.

A strong financial statement means that you've had a strong financial education.

The first part of a financial statement is the income statement. This is simply a representation of income from all sources compared to all expenses. The assumption is that the income portion is always larger than the expense portion—at least it should be. Unfortunately, research shows that many people in this country have that ratio reversed.[17]

The second part is the balance sheet, which represents assets and liabilities. According to Investopedia, the definition of an asset is, "a resource with economic value that an individual, corporation, or country owns or controls with the expectation that it will provide a future benefit." (Stuff you own that is worth something.) A liability is defined as someone's "legal, financial debts and obligations." (Debts that you owe to others.)

I prefer the simple, functional definition, coined by Robert Kiyosaki, who states, "Assets put money in your pocket and liabilities take money from your pocket." A strong balance sheet shows an abundance of assets compared to liabilities. That receives a "high grade" in the world of money.

Do you have a balance sheet? List your assets and resist the urge to count your golf clubs—they are worthless. Then look at your liabilities. Liabilities include your home mortgage, your car payments, student debt, and any other loans or obligations that you must eventually discharge. The more positive the resulting number, the stronger your balance sheet.

How about your income statement? Have you categorized all your income sources? Can you log all your expenses, including the ones you don't think are important? If this exercise is done honestly and completely, many people find that their expenses almost match their income; in some cases, expenses will exceed income. While this doesn't seem possible, the widespread availability of easy credit has made this more common than you would expect.

Doctors are accustomed to getting better-than-average grades on most tests. A strong financial statement is heavy on income and assets and light on expenses and liabilities. In the world of the rich, how would you stack up?

> **▶ ACTION ITEM ◀**
> Create your financial statement. Get help from your accountant if necessary. To download a user-friendly template, go to www.richdoctor.com/tools

It's *How* You Make Your Money that Counts

How you make your income is as important as how much income you make. One of the consistent themes in this book is that money doesn't make you rich. You need additional ingredients to become truly rich. Two of these include time and choices, which can be affected by how you produce your income.

As doctors, we are paid for our service and our time. My understanding during medical school was that a surgeon was paid based on the type of procedure performed and non-surgeons were paid for seeing patients. I didn't understand the exact mechanism, but one thing I knew was that you got paid more if you did more surgeries or saw more patients. This was logical and seemed like a good way to make a lot of money. From my observation the doctors that trained me appeared to be wealthy.

However, something about that bothered me from the beginning and the feeling grew over time. I started to realize that if I became a busy doctor, I would make more money, but it would require more and more of my time. It appeared that the more successful I became, the less time I would have. That didn't make sense and was not what I wanted, which caused me to search for other options.

My dilemma was finally put into a more concrete context years later again thanks to Robert Kiyosaki. You already know the story of how we met after I read *Rich Dad Poor Dad*. Shortly after that, Robert came to Austin to give a talk. The subject was "The Cashflow Quadrant," which became the title of his next book.

Robert spoke to about 30 people that day. At one point, he turned to a clean page on his flip chart and drew the figure represented below. "This," he said, "is the Cashflow Quadrant." As soon as he explained what it represented, everything fell into place for me. I now understood my anxiety over how I was making money and my ambition to find another way. It was a simple graphic, but it changed my entire thought process and gave me clarity on my financial mission.

The Cashflow Quadrant™

CASHFLOW Quadrant was created by Robert Kiyosaki. To learn more about the power of CASHFLOW Quadrant, go to www.richdad.com. Used with permission of CASHFLOW Technologies, Inc. All rights reserved. This grant of permission is not an endorsement of Tom Burns, or the content of this book.

The Cashflow Quadrant highlights four categories of income: E—Employee, S—Self-Employed, B—Business Owner, and I—Investor. Each derives his or her income in a different way: an Employee works for someone else; the Self-employed works for himself; a Business Owner has people work for him; an Investor has money work for him. The Employee and the Self-employed are on the left side of the quadrant. This is where most of the world makes a living. The Business Owner and the Investor occupy the right side of the Quadrant. This is where true wealth and freedom are found.

How you make your income is as important as how much income you make.

To be fair, there are wealthy people in all four quadrants. In general, though, most people who are financially free have reached that status by eventually migrating to the right side of the Cashflow Quadrant and becoming Investors and/or Business Owners.

As I learned more, I found that each Quadrant lived a different lifestyle. I was stuck in the "Self-employed Quadrant" where my time was required and if I didn't get out, I would never achieve my personal dreams and goals. I needed to get to the right side of the Quadrant and become an Investor. I wanted my money to work *for* me, thereby freeing up more of my time. With that time, I would be free to travel the world, be with my family, and pursue projects I was passionate about. I was ready to become a rich doctor.

Turning Point

My introduction to the Cashflow Quadrant was an important turning point for me. Every desire I had felt up to that point became justified and crystallized. I never wanted to work for someone else, so I became a self-employed doctor. That seemed like a great way to make money and I could call my own shots, but I soon discovered that plan would not give me the freedom I craved.

I saw doctors working long hours to maintain their lifestyle while internet start-ups were creating millionaires by the dozen. As the owners of these dotcoms built their companies and sold them, they became investors with all the time and freedom in the world to do what they wanted.

Up until this point I had one guiding thought about money: The harder you work, the more you make. I was a doctor making good money and getting busier and busier. When I looked at the Cashflow Quadrant, I saw that the people on the left side could make a lot of money but were forced to continually produce effort to do so. When I looked at the right side, I realized that while it might be a little harder to do at first, once the work was done, the money kept flowing without much effort—and without my time. That's what I wanted.

What do you want? Are you working for the sake of working, or do you have goals and dreams you would like to pursue? I can tell you the time passes quickly. Those of you who are older understand what I mean; the younger people reading this book will soon learn. The time is now to learn to make money work for you and give you the time to live your life as you desire.

As I became more familiar with this conceptualization of how we make money, my plan became clearer. I decided to become an investor. It fit my lifestyle and I didn't need to give up my mission as a doctor. I could simply add this skill to what I already knew and become a rich doctor. That's the plan we will talk about throughout the rest of this book.

Beware the Wall Street Mystique

When I was a young physician, I was told to make a lot of money, buy a big house, pay it off and give the rest to a "professional" money manager to invest. This advice came from just such a fellow who was hosting a "free" dinner for doctors. The premise was that a big house would protect my wealth since (at least in my state) a personal residence was shielded in bankruptcy and litigation, and of course only a professional (like our host) could manage my money properly.

At the time it seemed like prudent advice and I started on that path, but things soon changed. First, I have always had trouble delegating (a typical doctor disease!) and wanted to know how to do it myself. Second, I found that most of these financial planners had less money than I did and couldn't teach me how to be rich. They were just like me, making fees for their work.

I also noticed that they never advised me to sell. If the market went up, they told me to keep buying (and they got paid). If the market went down, they'd say "stay in for the long run" (and they got paid). Their fees were not tied to performance and the longer they controlled my money, the more they made for themselves. They weren't investing alongside me and I was the only one putting money at risk.

I have nothing against financial planners. If you want to be in the market and you don't have the expertise, they can be your guide. I have plenty of friends and relatives who are caring and ethical financial advisors. It's not the advisor who's the problem; it's the system. Newsflash: a financial advisor's primary duty is to make money for their firm, not for you. If they can make a profit for you, that is icing on the cake. They offer sanitized investments that protect them and their companies from liability but don't necessarily make you rich.

As the client, you are sometimes viewed only as a means of income. In his newsletter, Strategic Intelligence, Agora Financial's Jim Rickards discusses a looming stock market crash and states, "Professionals understand this, but don't care; they make good money in the meantime on commissions or wealth management wrap fees and invest their own money in ways quite different from those they advise clients."[18] Sobering words indeed.

A financial advisor's primary duty is to make money for their firm, not for you.

How many of you have been told to protect your retirement by "investing" in the stock market? It seems logical and beats blowing all your money or putting it under a mattress. If the market is kind to you, your money will grow over time. However, when I was young, it seemed that the *only* way to invest was in the stock market. This is certainly reinforced every day on television. You can't get through a Sunday morning without seeing a dozen television commercials from Wall Street investment firms extolling the virtues of their service. It's not bad advice—but it's not the only option.

Today I see posts on physician Facebook groups in which doctors state they are ready to invest and ask which stocks or mutual funds to buy. Some even consider real estate, but their first question is usually which real estate *fund* they should buy shares in, rather than what type of real property they should explore. It gives the impression that the stock market is considered the standard and every other form of investing is a departure from the norm, or too risky to take seriously.

I've spoken personally to physicians for years about investing. Often, they will proudly say that they are investors because they "have a guy" who takes care of that for them. They want to "leave the investing to the professionals." When asked about other investments, I usually get blank stares as if it's unfathomable to think that anything exists beyond the confines of Wall Street.

The stock market is a reasonable place to put some of your money, but it is not designed to make outsiders rich. It is manipulated and you have no control.

By the time a stock or mutual fund offering reaches a retail buyer, most of the money has already been made. The selling shareholders make the money on the initial offering. The investment bankers make money whether the offering is successful or not. Large insider institutions and individuals make the initial profits after the first purchase of the shares. Only then is it released to the unsuspecting public after all the cream has been pulled off the top. Profit can still be made, but you are last in line.

Wouldn't you rather be in the front of the line?

Average Returns

According to Nerdwallet.com, the S&P 500 has provided an average return of "about 10 percent annually" over the last century.[19] This seems like a comforting number and it is often quoted by financial firms. At that rate, most reasonable people would assume you can put your money in the market and can expect that return. However, these figures can be deceiving. It's in your best interest to know the real return you are getting on your money and what kind of fees you are paying.

The first thing to know is that this number doesn't account for inflation. The article goes on to state that inflation of 2-3 percent would bring that average return down to 7-8 percent. (Average inflation over the past 100 years was 3.22 percent.[20])

As for those "average returns," if the market goes down 10 percent this year and up 10 percent next year, that's a 0 percent average return, correct? Not so fast. Assume you have $100,000 in your account and you lose 10 percent. That leaves you with $90,000. Next year the market goes up 10 percent, which leaves you with $99,000. That's not a 0 percent return; it's a 1 percent loss.

Now let's consider brokerage fees applied to the same example. Most "averages" you see published do not take brokerage fees into account. With just a 1 percent fee on your initial $100,000 investment, the two-year scenario listed above would leave you with $97,030, because the fee is applied to both years. This *triples* your loss to 3 percent while the published average would be represented as 0 percent.

Year	Beg. Of Year Acct Value	Earnings Rate	Interest Earnings	End of Year Acct Value	Fees	Final Acct Value
1	$100,000	(10%)	($10,000)	$90,000	(900.00)	$89,100
2	$89,100	10%	$8,910	$98,010	(980.00)	$97,030

These seem like small percentages, but they add up quickly over time and those "small" losses can decimate your long-term return. Over their lifetime, the average hard-working person can lose up to 30 percent of their earnings due to 401(k) fees.[21] Mutual fund fees include expense ratios, administrative fees, 12b-1 fees, and sales load fees, to name a few. These costs are often well over the 1 percent described above and can have a significant negative effect on your portfolio. Some of those fees are listed below.

List of Mutual Fund Fees	
Shareholder fees	**0 - 8.5%**
Sales load fees	
Redemption fee	
Exchange fee	
Account fee	
Purchase fee	
Annual fund operating expenses	**1 - 3%**
Management fees	
12b1 fees	
Other expenses	

Data Source: https://www.sec.gov/files/ib_mutualfundfees.pdf

In his book, *Heads I Win, Tails You Lose*, CEO and author Patrick Donohoe provides a concise and understandable illustration of average returns and why they aren't what you think. He goes into great depth on where your hard-earned money really goes when you blindly give it to Wall Street. It's a must read if you want to be a good steward of your money.

Ask Your Hairdresser

If you have a good financial advisor, you don't have to know all this stuff, right? Again, not so fast. According to John McGregor, founder of ThrivePath and author of *The Top 10 Reasons the Rich Go Broke*, "This is a very common problem—people do little or no due diligence when selecting their advisor. They ask very few questions, never check referrals, never drill down. They go to the free chicken dinner and are ready to sign up immediately."

MacGregor, who *is* a financial planner, goes on to say, "It takes six weeks to pass your advisor exams and suddenly you're a Financial Advisor. It takes 18-24 months to become a hairdresser. People want to turn their money over to 'a professional' as quickly as possible, get back to their job, turn a blind eye—and hope for the best. They see a nice-looking advisor or team, well-dressed staff, nice offices with plaques on the wall, a big leather chair, and they're sold. Here's my money—take care of it for me."

It's like closing your eyes while a freight train is barreling down at you. Even if you don't watch, you're still going to get run over! Go to school, get a good job, buy on credit, and contribute to your 401(k). Eat your vegetables, brush your teeth, follow the crowd, and give your money to Wall Street. It's a herd mentality.

We are told the market is safe and liquid. We are told to be patient and invest for the long term. The advisor wears a nice suit and everybody does it, so it must be safe, right?

Ninety to Nothing

In 1985, an energy-trading company named Enron was formed after the merger of two gas companies. They quickly became the darling of the energy sector. Investors piled onto their shares and the stock climbed. Enron stock was owned by large pension funds, mutual funds, and millions of individuals. Everybody was getting rich.

By 2000, the company employed 21,000 people and was a Top Ten Fortune 500 Company.[22] At that time, their stock was over $90/share. A year later it had plummeted to $0.26/share. An SEC investigation eventually revealed that Enron had falsified its financial position and covered up billions of dollars of debts and losses.

The two top executives, Kenneth Lay and Jeffrey Skilling, were charged with conspiracy and fraud. Lay died of a heart attack, Skilling went to jail, and a lot of investor money was lost. This was a sensational story and the world was glued to the TV as they watched the executives get cuffed in their homes and hauled away to jail.

What gets overlooked is that half of the Wall Street "professional analysts" who covered Enron were still issuing "Buy" ratings as the stock plummeted, executives were arrested, and the SEC investigated![23] Consider that the next time you think a "professional" will take care better care of your money than you.

One story that didn't reach the media was that of my friend's father, who was an Enron engineer. As one of 21,000 employees, his retirement plan was wrapped up in the company's shares and stock options. During the good times, his retirement nest egg was growing by leaps and bounds. He was thinking about retiring early, traveling the world, buying a ranch, and living a relaxing life with his wife. When Enron collapsed, he lost it all. In a period of days, his retirement went from millions to almost nothing.

This was a real person and not a statistic, one of thousands whose lives were forever altered due to the greed of others. The sad part is they were following the conventional wisdom: "Work hard, save your money, and invest in the stock market for the long term."

How would your life be affected if your nest egg was wiped out just before you retired? Do you have a back-up plan?

Know Your Options

Bad things happen on Wall Street, but also in real estate and in other investments. No asset is immune. The point is that we are indoctrinated into thinking that all investing must be through traditional channels and that everything will be okay. Investing in stocks can be part of your wealth plan but be cautious about making it your only strategy.

In saying all this, my goal is merely to educate and stimulate you to think about your current plan. If you are seeking financial freedom, it helps to know how the system works and who the system is designed to benefit. You can make some money in paper markets, but the insiders will make much more whether the market goes up or down. If you are in for the "long term," you'll make money when the market goes up and lose it when it goes down.

Rich doctors are truly diversified when it comes to investing and consider all options.

Investing in stocks can be part of your wealth plan but be cautious about making it your only strategy.

Bad Guys in Disguise

June 29, 2009. Bernie Madoff, chairman of Madoff Investment Securities, was sentenced to 150 years in prison for orchestrating the largest Ponzi scheme in history.[24, 25] The size of the fraud was estimated at roughly $65 billion. Prior to the fall, Madoff was one of the top market makers on Wall Street and investors were "honored" to be in his fund. He was the talk of the town for twenty years. The media, his friends, and his investors felt he could do no wrong until the two-decade fraud was exposed. People's lives were, again, shattered.

Bad guys don't just inhabit Wall Street. Years ago, I was approached to lend short-term money for a real estate development to a well-known and well-connected person in the Texas state government. He was brought to me by a trusted friend. Before I agreed to the transaction, I called another well-connected friend who was high up in the Texas power structure. He said my proposed borrower was "the salt of the earth and a fine, church-going man!" Assuming I had done proper due diligence, I made the loan.

Almost immediately, I had to press him for the quarterly interest payments. After months of frustration, I demanded a loan payoff. He responded by putting a check in my mailbox, which was literally written in crayon! I called his bank and they said he didn't have the funds to cover that check. It turns out that he had everyone fooled. He was a colossal con man. He had stiffed dozens of high-powered and notable people for way more than my six-figure loan. The good news is that I was the only one who had structured interest payments into our contract, so at least I got something that the rest of his creditors did not. The last I heard, he was in jail.

I share these cautionary tales to make you aware that even if everyone around you has bought into a certain reality, it may not be so. Physicians are often prey to these types of criminals. I want you to learn from my mistakes, not yours, and hopefully you will never be burned by one of these scoundrels.

Doctor Watch Your Back

I was once told that everyone has an agenda. It may be a good one or a bad one, but your counterpart often isn't thinking about you. If he can help you and, in turn, help himself, then you have a good situation. If he can screw you to help himself, you could be in trouble.

Sadly, doctors are often targeted by the "ethically challenged." Throughout my seminar-attending career, I've been present at talks in which the man at the front of the room said this: "If you are just starting out, go for the doctors. They have money, they think they know everything, but they are unsophisticated in business." Ouch!

In a recent article on young doctors, their current debt level, and their lack of financial education, Johns Hopkins business professor and physician financial advocate, Yuval Bar-Or stated, "Young physicians are relentlessly pursued by financial product salespeople who often don't have doctors' best interests at heart."[26] Ouch again!

The bottom line is that you're an expert in your field, but when it comes to your money, there are plenty of expert scammers who wouldn't think twice about taking it from you.

Are doctors the only group with a dollar sign on their backs? Hardly. The bad guys are everywhere and have no bias as to who they get their money from. Physicians are simply more susceptible because they have little financial training and are typically in high-income brackets.

Here is one of my trophy examples. I walked into my orthopedic office break room one day and there were two gentlemen in suits who had brought lunch. Usually this translated to pharmaceutical or surgical implant salesmen. To my surprise, they said they were in real estate. Although I had been in commercial real estate for twenty years, I kept that to myself to see how they presented their product. At least they were showing some creativity!

I grabbed a sandwich and sat down. One of them opened the most beautiful 8.5 x 11 tri-fold brochure I had ever seen. (A friend of mine says, "The prettier the brochure, the worse the deal!") They were pitching the development of an apartment complex which, coincidentally, is what my real estate firm specializes in. So I asked a few basic industry questions and these guys couldn't answer them. They said they were the owners, developers, and builders and yet they knew none of the terms I was using.

I was getting frustrated because I saw big risk, unrealistic predictions, and no downside protection for the investor. Eventually, without giving any back-up, they said, "The numbers don't matter. You will triple your money in three years. We are going to sell for a huge profit!"

I knew that wasn't feasible, excused myself, and later checked their background. They were neither owners, builders, nor developers. They were hired salesmen and got paid based on how much money they raised. It didn't matter to them if the project failed because they were working for commissions. They were fishing in the doctor pond for "easy money" and they were dishonest about their role.

The bottom line is that you're an expert in your field, but when it comes to your money, there are plenty of expert scammers who wouldn't think twice about taking it from you. So watch your back and get educated, or get help.

Money Doesn't Play Favorites

Money doesn't care if you're the top doctor or live in a cardboard box. It doesn't care about race, color, religion, or educational level. It won't give you a break if you don't know the rules. It's a heartless beast that will swallow you up if you don't understand the game. But it's a fabulous employee if you know how to use it.

Just because we chose to be physicians, we have no greater right to become wealthy than anyone else in the world. On the other hand, because we are physicians, we have some advantages. We have the means to make financial mistakes and recover from them. We have money to invest. We have the resources to pay for our financial education. Take those benefits and use them to your advantage. Done right, you'll create personal financial freedom, options you never thought possible, and the chance to serve the rest of the world. That's what a true rich doctor does!

In the financial world, those with the gold make the rules. Who makes the rules in your world? Do they benefit you? Hopefully in this chapter you've learned a few of them. When you know the rules, it's easier to play the financial game and mine that gold.

BUILDING YOUR
PASSIVE INCOME PIPELINE

YOUR
NOW

YOUR
FUTURE

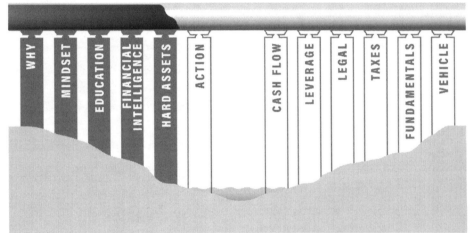

Chapter 7

Understand Money, Inflation and Hard Assets

A nickel ain't worth a dime anymore.

—Yogi Berra

Ｔhe dollar or the euro in your pocket isn't money, it's currency. It doesn't have intrinsic value. It's only a *representation* of value based on faith in governments and monetary systems. If that currency is only as valuable as we say it is, how truly safe is it? How long can we guarantee its worth?

The Dollar Decline

What is money? It's a medium of exchange, a unit of measurement, and a storehouse of value. It's how we obtain things we need. Everybody wants money, but what are you getting when someone hands you a coin or a note?

There are primarily two mediums of exchange: *commodity* money and *fiat* currency.

Commodity money is backed by something of tangible value and can be traded for that valuable item. The most recent form of commodity money was backed by gold. Prior to 1971, you could take your U.S. dollar and trade it for an equivalent amount of gold. This changed abruptly in 1971 when President Nixon took the United States off the gold standard.[27]

This caused the U.S. dollar to become fiat currency. The value of fiat currency is based on supply and demand as well as the world's faith in its worth. Without tangible backing such as gold, the value of fiat currency can be manipulated.

Enter the central banks of the world such as the U.S. Federal Reserve, the European Central Bank and the People's Bank of China, who can now control the money supply with a mere flip of a switch. If they want the money to be more valuable, they will decrease the supply. If they desire cheap money, they will flood the market. During the Great Recession in 2008 and beyond, central banks lowered interest rates from 5.25 percent to 0 percent while the Federal Reserve injected trillions of dollars into the financial system.[28] This increased the money supply which, in turn, lowered the value of the currency.

Without tangible backing such as gold, the value of fiat money can be manipulated.

Today the U.S. money supply is overseen by the Federal Reserve Board, created in 1913 by President Woodrow Wilson.[29] Since then, it has used its powers to stabilize the ups and downs of the U.S. economy and they were on full display in the form of "Quantitative Easing" (QE) during the Great Recession. Since that time, the government has created almost $4 trillion of excess liquidity out of thin air to avoid another collapse of the financial system. (As this book went to press, the Fed was lowering rates and the government was injecting more money into the system in response to a worldwide virus pandemic.)

While there have been benefits to this easily manipulated system, it has had a relentless, long-term, dampening effect on the U.S. dollar and its buying power. As more money is produced, the value of the dollar declines. Since 1913, the U.S. dollar has lost 96 percent of its buying power![30]

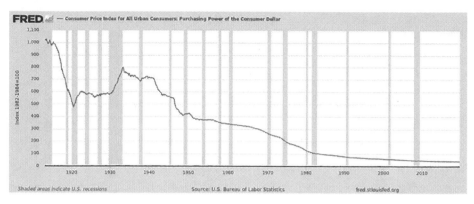

Source: fred.stlouisfed.org

Inflation

This loss of buying power is what we call inflation; it is incessant, persistent, and insidious. You can feel its effect in everyday life. Almost anything that you bought ten or twenty years ago costs more today than it did then. Car prices go up every year. Groceries cost more. Housing becomes more and more expensive.

Sometimes inflation escalates out of control. At the beginning of World War I, for example, Germany took its currency off of the gold standard and soon it began to devalue. In 1918, less than one German mark bought a dozen eggs. A mere five years later, those same eggs cost four billion marks![31]

In 2005, I was in Zimbabwe on a safari. When it came time to leave a tip, I was informed by the guide that the tips had to be paid in Zimbabwe dollars. He had the local currency ready to exchange for my U.S. dollars. I gave him $2,000 and he opened a briefcase and handed me three million Zimbabwe dollars—the result of 1,000 percent inflation. I felt like a big tipper that day! Sadly, the currency collapsed over the next three years and reached a monthly percentage inflation rate into the billions![32]

The salient point to grasp is that inflation is always present. Products and services don't become inherently more valuable over time. A steak is a steak; it doesn't gain value from year to year, but it takes more and more currency to buy that steak because the currency you are using has less value. This loss of value is inflation and it's a covert wealth stealer. In the words of former U.S. President Ronald Reagan, "Inflation is as violent as a mugger, as frightening as an armed robber, and as deadly as a hit man."

This is an important concept if you want to become rich. What would happen if you had placed a $100 bill under your mattress in 1914 and tried to spend it today? It would still be a $100 bill, so it should buy $100 worth of goods, correct? Yes, but the composition of those goods has changed. According to the *Farmers' Almanac*, in 1914 that $100 would buy you 1,667 loaves of bread.[33] Today it will buy you 40 loaves. It's the same piece of paper, but its value—its buying power—has declined over time due to inflation.

	1914	2018
Car	$ 500	$ 35,285
House	$ 3,500	$ 222,800
Milk	$ 0.32	$ 3.50
Bread	$ 0.06	$ 2.50
Gas	$ 0.12	$ 2.90

Data Source: Farmers' Almanac

Why should the price of a loaf of bread, or a steak dinner interest you? This lesson on inflation helps to explain why the rich stay rich and why sometimes you feel like you're never getting ahead. The dollar you earn today is worth less tomorrow and even less the next day. Its purchasing power keeps declining. If you are a doctor, and you rely almost exclusively on income that comes in dollars, this is happening to you now, right under your nose.

According to the Medicare Physician Fee Schedule, physician payment increased 2.5 percent from 2006 to 2017. During that same time, inflation went up 23 percent.[34] This means that if you did the same amount of work during that 11-year period, you would have suffered a 20.5 percent pay cut. Your salary would have essentially been "put under the mattress" for eleven years and now it buys less than it did before.

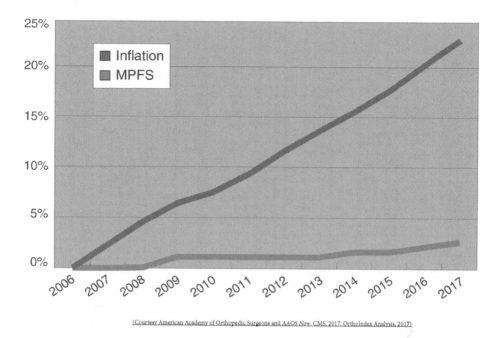

(Courtesy American Academy of Orthopedic Surgeons and *AAOS Now*. CMS, 2017; OrthoIndex Analysis, 2017)

Those are staggering numbers if you think about it. Just to keep up with inflation, you would have had to boost your revenue 2 percent *each year* above and beyond any salary increases. That's easier said than done. Unlike the Federal Reserve, you can't just give yourself a raise or magically produce money out of thin air. Your revenue is determined by corporations and insurance companies and you are not permitted to raise your prices. If you want more money, you will need to work more, which takes more of your precious time.

If you've been in practice for more than ten years, you can probably look back and see the slow lifestyle changes that have occurred—and perhaps the source of that nagging feeling that you can't get ahead. Even though you've marketed to bring in new patients and added practice-related profit centers, at best you were only able to maintain the status quo. Your office rent increases, your employees get raises, and supply prices go up every year. Yet the insurance companies or your employers don't raise your revenue so you can keep up. I know all this is true because it happened in my own practice!

For physicians as well as many other types of professionals, this is the curse of inflation.

So, is inflation bad? It depends on your point of view. If your income is based on a fixed amount of currency (e.g., dollar amount), then inflation will gradually erode your buying power. Left unchecked, this will eventually have a negative effect on your lifestyle. But some investments actually rise in value (in currency terms), keeping pace with or even exceeding inflation. As you will see below, some asset types help protect against inflation.

A rich doctor uses inflation as a component of a wealth-building strategy. A poor doctor becomes its victim!

You can also use inflation to your advantage when it comes to paying for these investments. In simple terms, you often pay for them over time by borrowing money. One benefit of using intelligently borrowed money is that, while your asset is becoming more valuable due to inflation, the dollars you use to pay for it are worth less each year due to that same inflation. As you learn about debt in a later chapter, you will discover how powerful this concept is. The moral of the story: A rich doctor uses inflation as a component of a wealth-building strategy. A poor doctor becomes its victim!

Four Asset Types

Now that you understand what money represents and how inflation affects it, you need to know how you want to make it and protect it. There are four broad categories of assets you can use to create your wealth: businesses, commodities, paper assets, and real estate. You may find that you match well with one or more of them. The key here is not so much the asset class but which one fits your psychological make-up, your lifestyle, and your goals. Each person has different aspirations and talents. As you read the broad descriptions below, try to identify which area or asset class fits you the best or gets you the most excited.

BUSINESS

There are 28 million small businesses in the United States.[35] They are the backbone of our economy. The American dream is to own your own business and produce a profit that covers your expenses with something left over for vacation and retirement. Ultimately, if it's a solid company, you may be able to sell it and pocket the profits.

Owning a business can be a true path to wealth, but it's difficult to establish and run a profitable company. According to the *Cashflow Quadrant™*, business ownership is on the right side of the quadrant and a tool of the rich, but running a successful company takes the highest level of financial education and can sap your time. The Small Business Administration confirms that half of all start-ups fail within the first five years, and only 33 percent make it to Year 10.[36]

Even if you lasted the first five years, there's no guarantee that the venture will be profitable. Compound that by trying to run a business as a busy physician. It's the rare doctor who can juggle those hours and has the background to run a successful company. I've seen it done, but usually there's a good partner or an efficient system to make that possible.

As an alternative to understanding and running a company, some doctors prefer to invest in businesses, especially medical start-ups. In the surgery world, we are constantly approached to help finance new medical device companies. Part of the pitch is getting titles such as "advisor" or "consultant" that ostensibly make us part of the company. These titles don't usually carry extra financial benefit, but psychologically they can make a physician feel special and more prone to give money. In my opinion, such an investment pitch is simply a hook used by salesmen to get access to equity, marketing, and channels for new leads.

Nevertheless, these companies are no different than any other start-up; they have the same chances of success or failure. Moreover, most physicians don't have the experience to assess the strength of a business plan, the manufacturing process, the management team, the distribution network, or the product. One of my colleagues invested in a company because he was familiar with the product and that made him feel comfortable. He was also convinced he was going to make a fortune. I've been told more than once by doctor friends that soon they "will never have to work another day in their lives." All of them are still working.

Forgive me if I seem blunt, but my objective is to give you as much information as possible to navigate the world of wealth. For some reason, these home run swings seem more attractive to doctors than boring, stable, good old cash flow. Invest in these companies if you wish but keep your eyes open and get some help from a third-party consultant. Ask your CPA to look at the financial statement and seek out someone in that field to give you an objective opinion about the company's business plan. I say this from experience. I didn't always do that and paid dearly when I didn't!

Owning a business is an option for working physicians either with partners or as an online venture. If you don't have partners or are also expected to provide some type of day-to-day service, prepare for either less sleep or the cannibalization of your professional time. You will have to make a choice.

Also, be wary of providing the capital, while someone else runs the company. There is nothing worse than having your money at risk, but not having control over the success or failure of the venture. I've been there, done that, and it was painful.

Don't get me wrong. Creating or owning a successful business is one of the best ways to become wealthy. Richard Branson, Sergey Brin and Jeff Bezos are among the wealthiest people in the world and there are many others. But it takes a solid team, a full-time commitment, and a significant amount of financial education. Most physicians don't have the luxury of possessing all those assets.

One final thought on business ownership as an asset class: In the early days of my financial journey, I felt I had that side of the equation covered. After all, I owned a medical practice with employees that provided a direct service to clients. But while I technically owned the company, it wasn't a true business.

A true business can eventually function and grow without the physical efforts of its owner(s). Even though I owned the company and wasn't an "employed physician," the practice was essentially worthless without me. I couldn't just sell it and move to Bali so I could free dive for oysters. It depended solely on my efforts for success. If I didn't see patients and keep producing revenue, the practice would fail. The reality was that I owned a job rather than a valuable business. In fact, I was the business! Don't fall into that trap.

COMMODITIES

Commodities are tradable assets with inherent value such as gold, oil, agricultural crops, and collectibles such as art or memorabilia. They are one of the favorite wealth preservation tools of the rich. When considering assets to hold, the rich choose commodities because they often remain stable over long periods of time. They think in terms of generations rather than next week's paycheck or retirement.

I have a friend who makes his money in the oil world. That's a great industry if you understand it the way he does. His excess cash is housed in real estate and a large collection of sports and music memorabilia. This sounds like a hobby but it's not.

Collectibles not only tend to maintain their worth but can grow in value at sometimes astonishing rates. Babe Ruth's 1920 jersey was last sold for $4.4 million.[37] In 2013, Pablo Picasso's *Le Reve* sold for $155 million.[38] My friend has a guitar signed by all four of the Beatles! Not a bad savings account if you can get it. Admittedly, collectibles are valued on a more emotional basis than other commodities, but some have withstood the test of time.

Because of their inherent or perceived value, commodities can be an excellent hedge against inflation. Remember, an item may not be worth more, but it might require more currency to buy it due to inflation. For this reason, a certain portion of a wealthy portfolio contains some exposure to these assets. Although not foolproof, it's somewhat of a safety net.

Ownership of commodities is not usually the first step to wealth creation, though. Typically, they are used to store or increase wealth created from other cash-flowing vehicles. However, if you are educated, you can produce cash flow by owning a producing oil well, or trading commodities. As your wealth and knowledge grows, they could become a valuable piece of your financial plan.

PAPER ASSETS

The most ubiquitous asset in the U.S. is paper, which consists of stocks, bonds, mutual funds, ETFs (exchange traded funds), and REITs (real estate investment trusts), to name a few.

My stock market exposure began in the typical fashion. Once I began to collect a paycheck, I sought out a financial planner and began putting my extra cash into the market. I used "dollar cost averaging" and put my kids' college money into mutual funds. Things were going well in the late 90s and my portfolio was growing.

Then I got greedy. People were trading stocks and making fortunes. I was in Austin, Texas, home of Dell computers, and every Dell employee was becoming rich. I had to get in on the action!

I began trading technology stocks that I knew nothing about. At first, I made money. Back then you could pick any tech stock on TV—companies like JDS Uniphase and Vignette —and it would go up within the next week or two. In 1999 you couldn't miss. Then the market crumbled in 2001 and I gave back almost all my profits. That's the story of an uneducated stock trader. I had no training in the industry and I was lucky to escape without a huge loss.

Investing and trading in paper assets can be an excellent way to grow your wealth, and produce cash flow, but it requires study, experience and discipline. I had none of those. The way it is depicted on television makes it look easy, but those ads are directed at the retail investor—the man (or woman) on the street.

The experts in paper investing use option strategies, fundamental and technical analysis, and rigid risk management. As is typical in the world of the rich, education and experience make this a valid strategy. If it does fit your personality and risk profile, I suggest you attend focused seminars on how to use the paper market to create wealth. There you'll be able to practice and learn before putting your money at risk. Remember, your education is a key component to your success and simulation is the best way to learn prior to doing the real thing.

Paper assets do play an important role in the global economy. The wealthiest people in the world house trillions of dollars in the financial markets. Our financial system couldn't function without the global markets. You couldn't get a good loan for your home if the equity and debt markets did not exist.

If you know what you're doing and have the proper training, you too can produce wealth with paper. If you have the right knowledge, you can also use paper assets to create a stable store of liquid cash which can be used when other opportunities arise.

REAL ESTATE

Real estate is difficult to discuss as one homogenous entity. It's not just "one thing." There are different types such as residential, commercial, hospitality, and industrial. These different sectors are dispersed across the world, and economic conditions vary by location. An apartment property in Cape Town, South Africa, does not compare to apartments in Austin, Texas, and neither one compares to a land purchase in Panama or office property in Memphis, Tennessee. Each is subject to unique laws and market dynamics. Success depends on your experience, location, and property focus. Sometimes I think that's the allure of participating in the property market; you have some control over your results.

As in any asset class, real estate can be good or bad depending on the market and your level of experience and education. While there is no "best" way to grow wealth, real estate is a solid enough investment that 10 percent of the world's billionaires made their money in property and the rich continue to invest in this asset class.[39, 40]

Real estate carries the benefits of asset appreciation, cash flow, generous government tax incentives, and the ability to use leverage—each of which will be explained in later chapters. I chose real estate because it fit my busy physician lifestyle. I didn't need to know everything, it moved slowly, I could use partners and it had a long track record of success. People will always need a place to live, work, or play. No new land is being manufactured, so supply is limited.

I've now been investing for my own account as well as for other investors for over 25 years. That experience has given me a relatively unique perspective on the relationship between professionals and real estate investing.

Real estate is a "hard asset." So are commodities such as oil, gold and some art. A hard asset retains its value in the face of currency fluctuations. Why is that important?

Why Hard Assets?

Over three years starting in 1929, the Dow Jones Industrial Average dropped 90 percent.[41] In one day on October 19, 1987, the Dow dropped 22.6 percent.[42] Over 18 months during the 2008 Great Recession, the Standard and Poor's 500 Index fell 56 percent.[43] The largest point drop in history occurred in March 2020, as this book was being written.[44] In some cases, it took years or decades for those markets to recover.

Scary! Those are infrequent events, but they do occur and can have a devastating impact on your lifestyle and financial security, if you rely too much on paper assets. Markets do recover, and if you have staying power, you can sometimes ride out the storm. But if you aren't liquid enough, life will get challenging. Wouldn't it be nice to feel confident that you have something that gives you a better chance of surviving such a calamity?

Hard assets provide diversification and a counterbalance against inflation.

That's why I preach the wisdom of understanding hard assets such as real estate, commodities, and certain businesses. A hard asset is something tangible that you can touch and feel. They aren't the only ways to invest, but they provide diversification, a counterbalance against inflation and preferably cash flow. And while they can all be affected by crashes; the value of physical assets typically doesn't drop to zero. By comparison, your stock holdings can go to zero and you have no control over them. Remember Enron!

During the Great Recession, stocks eventually fell 50 percent. During that same time, my real estate investments were affected, but most grew in value and some continued to produce cash flow. I was in control of my real estate assets but had no control over the stock market. I couldn't call Bill Gates and ask him to improve the profitability of Microsoft, but I could adjust my rents to keep my properties full in bad times.

Explore Your Options

There are plenty of ways to make money. Although the stock market is one option, I hope I've made clear that it's not the only way—neither is real estate, commodities, or business. Each sector has its strengths and weaknesses. More billionaires were created in finance and business than anywhere else but it's the riskiest path. When they do make their money, often they preserve it in hard assets.

And remember, no matter what asset type you use, it is only a true asset if it puts money in your pocket! Cash flowing rental property is an asset. Your golf clubs are not.

So, as you build your pipeline of passive income, seek out tangible assets that you can see, smell, and touch. For example, my real estate looks beautiful, my oil smells bad, and my gold feels great. Each one preserves my wealth and often creates more. I want you to experience the same level of comfort and confidence. It just requires a little knowledge, action, and persistence!

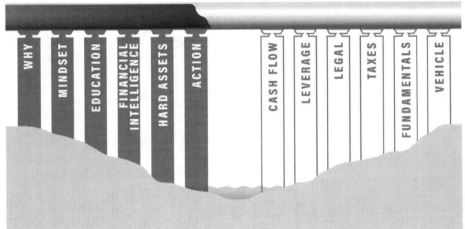

BUILDING YOUR
PASSIVE INCOME PIPELINE

YOUR
NOW

YOUR
FUTURE

WHY · MINDSET · EDUCATION · FINANCIAL INTELLIGENCE · HARD ASSETS · ACTION

CASH FLOW · LEVERAGE · LEGAL · TAXES · FUNDAMENTALS · VEHICLE

Chapter 8

Get in the Game

You miss 100 percent of the shots you don't take.

—WAYNE GRETZKY

By now you've learned the basics of what it takes to play the financial freedom game. You've determined why you want to be wealthy. You have a personal definition of what it means to be rich. You now know the wealthy don't work for money. You understand the mindset it takes to move forward and are changing your words and thoughts to do so. You know where to look for the education that will guide you down the path to financial freedom. Finally, you have a working knowledge of money and assets, and you've sharpened your financial intelligence. Pre-season is over, and you're ready to be a rich doctor. What's next?

Well, as my friends Russell Gray and Robert Helms, co-hosts of the top-rated The Real Estate Guys™ Radio Show say, "Education is great, but it is most powerful when combined with effective action." What you've learned will be refined and expanded by putting it to use in real situations. Metaphorically, you must put on your helmet on and get in the game!

If you put your wealth and your goals in someone else's hands, they will realize their dreams—not yours.

Unfortunately, this is where some people decide to stay on the sidelines. It's easy to gain some book knowledge but scary to put it into action. Don't let this happen to you! You will be tempted to take the easy path that follows conventional wisdom and requires no personal effort or courage. That route can be equally treacherous and unsafe as you get farther down the road. If you put your wealth and your goals in someone else's hands, they will realize their dreams—not yours. You owe it to yourself to create your own path.

Getting in the game is the transition from book learning to real education.

Start with Baby Steps

So how do you get started? The good news is that you've already begun. You had enough curiosity or discomfort to pick up this book and learn some information that would help you change something in your life. Psychologists tell us that humans act primarily based on the pursuit of pleasure or the avoidance of pain. Either emotion defines a desire to change one's environment. Your desire to change or improve your life is your first step.

The path may seem imposing, but as the ancient philosopher Lao Tzu said, "A journey of 1,000 miles begins with one step." I suggest you start small. This will create more victories and it's less costly. The good news is that, if you are a physician, you have an advantage over many others: An income that can absorb some of the mistakes you will inevitably make on this journey. You will learn from each small blunder so you can succeed when the stakes are higher.

I began the journey early. I was working in a profession I loved, but I knew it wouldn't last forever and I had a dream of financial independence. I didn't have knowledge or experience, so I simply took calculated risks. I won some and lost plenty but starting small kept me in the game because the losses weren't devastating.

Admittedly, I might be the poster boy for "attention deficit" in the world of passive income and I've explored plenty of options in the search for it. Many of those experiments failed. Some, however, bore fruit and have provided a secure and diverse income stream. The ones that worked are ones on which I direct my focus.

Again, there is no one "right way" to get in the game. You just have to go out there and skin your knee a few times. I assure you the scrapes will heal quickly, and the rewards will last a lifetime.

Find Your Niche

One of the first questions I always get is, "What should I invest in?" It's a question I never answer directly because the solution is different for everyone. There's a story about Einstein in which he gave his graduate students the same test in successive weeks. One of his colleagues asked him how and why he would give two tests with the exact same questions. Einstein answered, "Ah yes, the questions are the same, but the answers are different!" Keep this perspective in mind. The same investment opportunity can elicit entirely different reactions from people depending on who they are and what they want.

I chose the real estate world. There was a low barrier to entry, it moved slow, it could be managed part-time or full-time, and it could be done alone or with partners. This perfectly fit the lifestyle of a busy surgeon.

In the early days, I was tied up in my practice as an orthopedic surgeon from 6:00 am until 5:00 pm and often worked through the evenings on emergency cases. So, I had to find something that was compatible with my schedule and the real estate world gave me that flexibility.

I started small by purchasing properties that fit my budget. Over time, the properties I purchased became larger. During this process, I met other people who were on the same course as me. I partnered with some of them and eventually the projects became larger. Today those properties produce passive income that far outweighs my orthopedic income and easily takes care of my living and leisure expenses.

Real estate worked for me, but it might not fit your own unique talents or interests. I know plenty of physicians who've achieved some degree of financial freedom using other vehicles. A friend of mine was an ear, nose, and throat surgeon who retired from medicine by becoming a popular podcaster. A former obstetrician started a medical technology company and sold it. Another obstetrician became a UPS franchisee and now owns six stores. Quite a few others have found their financial footing online.

You can trade stock options, buy a franchise, start a company, become a blogger, invest in real estate, or choose one of the thousands of other ways to make money. The vehicle you choose is less important than making sure it's the right one for you. Once you decide, take action, follow the principles you learn from this book and become an expert in your niche.

Seek Mentors

Physicians are trained to have all the knowledge required to perform their duties. The final decision in the exam or operating room usually falls to us. We are trained to be self-sufficient and make the decisions necessary to treat illness and suffering. It's in our DNA to take full responsibility. We're supposed to be confident and have all the answers, and it can feel like weakness to ask for help and advice.

Stories of doctors finding a niche and creating a business can be intimidating. After all, it was hard enough to learn how to be a good doctor. How do we get all the answers to excel at something new? The good news is you don't have to. When you're traveling the road to financial freedom, you don't have to do it alone.

In the academic world, during test time, collaboration is considered cheating. In the world of money and business, it's routine to get help from others. When it comes to building your personal wealth, asking for help is not a sign of weakness and it's not cheating. It's smart and it's how to succeed. As one who struggled with this, I came to realize the value of others in helping me to achieve my dreams.

In the world of financial freedom, help often comes in the form of mentors. A mentor doesn't have to be older than you or smarter than you. A mentor is simply someone who has been where you'd like to go and is willing to draw on their experience to help you get there.

In my case, I sought out a friend who was a well-known real estate developer and said, "I like what you do. I'd like to learn it. Will you teach me?" He was a bit surprised, but he agreed. I worked with him for several years without pay but received a priceless education. An unexpected benefit of that mentorship was the eventual development of a multi-building medical office complex and full-service hospital—all because I first sought guidance.

A mentor is simply someone who has been where you'd like to go and is willing to draw on their experience to help you get there.

You are the expert in your field. People seek you out for opinions and advice. But we can't be all things. As you formulate and implement your plan, find others who have the expertise you need or have reached a goal that you desire. There are generous people around every corner; you merely have to seek them out. Some may charge you, but if you must pay, consider it an investment in the future you. What better place to put your money?

Find Partners

While mentors are important for education and oversight, having a partner can accelerate your progress and multiply your capabilities. Although I had a nicely performing portfolio of real estate properties that I'd purchased on my own, more success came through partnering with some great people. That medical office project mentioned above would never have happened without the help of a mentor who became—and still is—a partner. I couldn't have done it alone, nor could I have reached this scale of commercial development without his guidance and friendship.

I met my second business partner at a seminar in Phoenix. Soon after that he moved to my town and we started to do some deals together. That led to our first large project in 2010 and since then, we've been close friends and loyal teammates. I believe my life and my financial condition were enriched by having him as a friend and business partner.

I can't say enough about the value of having a good partner, but it may take you a while to find one. I would love to say that the people above have been my only partners, but in truth they are the only ones I would trust with my money. I've had other partners who didn't turn out so well. So, while I strongly recommend the importance they can play, there are some things you should know before committing to a business partnership. These tips will help you avoid some of the mistakes I've made:

1. Perform your due diligence. Talk to previous associates, get bank statements and tax returns if possible, and do a background check. If your potential partner won't allow that level of transparency, you might be better served looking for someone else to work with.

2. Sign written agreements, prepared by an attorney, with your partner. Handshake agreements are great and can work. But when money is involved and if things go bad, memories fade and the good intentions of that original palm slap are quickly forgotten.

3. Add "divorce" provisions in your agreement. If you have irreconcilable differences with your partner, you can more easily unwind the company with a prior agreement that anticipates this possibility.

4. Be a good partner and expect your counterpart to do the same. Honesty and transparency always beat collusion and selfishness.

Seek Associations

As mentioned in a previous chapter, you become the average of the five people you associate with the most. If you hang around successful, energetic people, that alone will help you sustain the motivation and passion to keep you moving forward. You can often find these people in organized groups or loose associations of like-minded folks.

Multiple industries have meet-up groups and associations. There are Facebook groups for almost everything. LinkedIn has hundreds of industry groups. You can search both by keywords that relate to your special interest. Often, these social media groups are augmented with live meetups. In all these places, you can learn about your chosen industry, meet potential mentors and partners, and find opportunities to reach your goals.

> **▶ ACTION ITEM ◀**
> Search social media and network with friends to find groups that share your interests.

We talked about seminars in the "education" chapter. Not only are they an excellent place to get the information you need; it's where you can form friendships and create potential partnerships. Those who attend seminars are usually a self-selected group of people who have decided to make a change in their lives and are likely on a journey just like yours. Find those people and get in the game!

Bucket of Crabs

Have you heard the story of the bucket of crabs? It goes like this: One sunny afternoon, a man was walking along the beach and saw another man fishing in the surf with a bait bucket beside him. As he drew closer, he saw that the bait bucket had no lid and had live crabs inside. "Why don't you cover your bait bucket, so the crabs won't escape?" he asked. "You don't understand." the man replied, "If there is one crab in the bucket it would surely crawl out very quickly. But when there are many crabs in the bucket, if one tries to crawl up the side, the others will grab hold of it and pull it back down so that it shares the same fate as the rest of them."

When you start the ascent to *your* goal, some will try to pull you down. They won't understand why a doctor would want or need financial freedom. You'll be told to focus on medicine, that patients should come first, that you are throwing your training away. Nothing could be further from the truth. Because of my freedom, I've been able to focus more intently on my patients and spend even more time with them. I have the freedom to treat them for free if needed. I can use my training for its highest and best use.

---

*I know that financial freedom will transform your life, but
I believe thousands of doctors with financial freedom can
change the world.*

I want the same for you and your patients. You can be free to create your own destiny. Some of you will leave medicine, but many will seek out humanitarian efforts, and others will work to eradicate diseases and conditions that currently have no cures. That's the real victory. Personal happiness is a worthwhile goal, but we have the potential to have a global impact. I know that financial freedom will transform your life, but I believe thousands of doctors with financial freedom can change the world.

While I can't promise the path will be easy, I can assure you that the rewards will last a lifetime. As Theodore Roosevelt said, "The credit belongs to the man who is in the arena…so that his place shall never be with those cold and timid souls who neither know victory nor defeat." So get in the game and build *your* life; leave the crabs in the bucket.

PART III

How to Become a Rich Doctor

Twenty years from now you will be more disappointed by the things that you didn't do than by the ones you did do.

—MARK TWAIN

BUILDING YOUR
PASSIVE INCOME PIPELINE

YOUR
NOW

YOUR
FUTURE

> > > PASSIVE INCOME

WHY

MINDSET

EDUCATION

FINANCIAL INTELLIGENCE

HARD ASSETS

ACTION

CASH FLOW

LEVERAGE

LEGAL

TAXES

FUNDAMENTALS

VEHICLE

Chapter 9

Make Money Work for You

If you don't find a way to make money while you sleep,
you will work until you die.

—WARREN BUFFETT

In the first year of my private practice career, I was talking with another orthopedic surgeon who was about 10 years older than me. He was one of the busiest guys in town and did an extraordinary amount of surgery each week. He drove a luxury car and was building a huge house in the nicest part of town. All the hospitals loved him because he brought in lots of profitable business. As a young, ambitious physician, I was openly envious of his success.

Then he told me something I will never forget. It changed the course of my life as a doctor and as a father.

He said he had worked hard to build his business during the first 10 to 15 years of his career and that it took sacrifice and hard work. He then lamented that part of the sacrifice was not seeing his family as often as he would have liked. He never really had a chance to watch his children grow up or develop a close relationship with them.

Now they were teenagers and he was trying to reestablish a connection with them. He said it was painful and not going well. His eyes filled with tears as he expressed his fear that it may be too late. He said he had traded a precious part of his life for his professional success and was worried he would never get it back.

This hit me like a ton of bricks. We had a three-year-old daughter and my wife and I were about to have a second child. Shivers went down my spine as I imagined not being close with my children or trying to live with the fact that they didn't know me or want to be with me.

Almost immediately I started noticing people in other professions who were married to their work and missed a lot of their kids' activities. They didn't like it but felt that it was their only choice. I then made a vow that I would never put money in front of family. I had to find a way to succeed without making them sacrifice. I would not trade my life with them just to make money.

Trading Time for Money

Most people in the world are paid by the hour or by the job. According to the *Bureau of Labor Statistics*, the median hourly wage for carpenters in 2018 was $22.40, while the average hourly wage for an orthopedic surgeon was $230.[45, 46] Orthopedic surgeons are often called the "carpenters" of medicine, so why the discrepancy?

I once heard that you are paid according to the degree of complexity of the problems you solve. Solving medical problems is a complex process and requires years of training, so the pay scale for a surgeon is higher than that of a carpenter. While the doctor brings home ten times the carpenter's salary, the two jobs carry one important similarity: Both require trading time and effort for money. The carpenter and the surgeon *actively* produce their income.

The production of active income requires time and is the way most of the world makes its money. Whether you're a CEO, surgeon or grocery clerk, you don't get paid unless you give your time and effort to a prescribed task. We will all do what we must to provide for our families, but the cost can be high. Time is our most precious commodity and we only have a limited amount to give. Once it is gone, we never get it back.

How do we solve this conundrum? *Passive income.*

In order to create a life of true financial freedom, you must develop some level of *passive* income. This is income that comes in whether you work or not and does not require your physical input or your time. With the right amount of passive income, you can free your time to pursue your passions. When you control your time, your control your life.

In order to create a life of true financial freedom, you must develop some level of passive income.

Henry David Thoreau once said, "The price of anything is determined by the amount of life you are willing to trade for it." Are you trading a portion of your life that you would rather use for other activities? Is it your goal to be "busy" just to make a living, or would you rather have a life that is meaningful with plenty of time for the things you love? If you could produce the income you desire without having to trade your time, would that improve your life?

The answers to these questions seem easy, but after years of thinking we must work for money, the thought process is hard to break.

The Power of Passive Income

Years ago, I was in the doctors' lounge between surgery cases when another surgeon asked about some of my real estate projects. Since he asked, I told him I was working on a project I thought would be successful. It required an investment of $100,000 and, after one year of no return, it would provide $1,000 per month of income in perpetuity or until the asset sold.

Surprisingly, this bothered the surgeon. He couldn't see why he had to wait a year to get paid. In addition, while this wasn't pocket change, he said $1,000 a month wouldn't significantly change his life. Finally, he said, "I can just work one day a month in the emergency room and make that much money."

I then asked him what he would do the next month to make that $1,000. He said he'd work another day in the emergency room. I asked about the next month and the one after that, but he never really got the point, which was that he would need to trade time *every month* to make that $1,000.

He never quite understood that, with the right investment, he could do the work once and be paid forever with no additional effort. Needless to say, he didn't invest in my deal.

If you always trade your time for money, you will always be required to work.

While this doctor knew how to make active income, he failed to grasp the awesome power of passive income. He didn't fully understand that if you always trade your time for money, you will always be required to work. This takes precious time away from the things that mean most to you in life.

We have a huge advantage as highly paid doctors. We have the opportunity to turn our excess cash into perpetual passive income. This is money produced on a recurring basis without the physical or mental effort of the receiver. This is how the wealthy produce their fortunes. They don't work for money. Money works for them—24/7. It's the magic formula for financial freedom. It creates rich doctors.

The Magic Formula

Thankfully, I understood the logic of passive income early in my career. I wanted income that wasn't dependent on me being there to produce it. I just didn't know what to call it yet or how to make it happen. But when I saw a simple graphic in a book, my financial goals finally crystallized.

The figure reproduced below from *Rich Dad Poor Dad* depicts a basic financial statement. Its simplicity is its brilliance. The income statement is represented by the two boxes on top, the balance sheet by the two boxes on the bottom. Typically, money flows into the income box and goes out the expense box. Assets put money in the income box and liabilities take it out of the expense box.

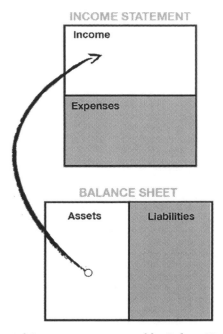

CASHFLOW Financial Statement was created by Robert Kiyosaki. To learn more about the power of CASHFLOW Financial Sheet, go to www.richdad.com. Used with permission of CASHFLOW Technologies, Inc. All rights reserved. This grant of permission is not an endorsement of Tom Burns, or the content of this book.

In the example above, the money flowing into the income box doesn't require ongoing effort to produce. It's *passive income.* I knew this was how I would attain my freedom. This mechanism would allow me to pursue my dreams. I would no longer be required to be in an office or an operating room to feed my family. Those assets would be working for me no matter where I was or what I was doing.

Once I understood that, life got really simple. Since 1997, when I stayed up all night and read *Rich Dad Poor Dad* from cover to cover, my sole financial goal was to fill that asset box. It didn't matter what it was. If it produced income, even just a few dollars, it went into the box. If I didn't have to physically work to produce income, it went into the box. I wanted passive income to replace my active income.

This was 20 years before Gary Keller's book, *The One Thing*, but passive income became my "one thing." It removed the guesswork and hesitancy from my plan. I knew what I was looking for and could eliminate projects that didn't fit the plan.

Things moved slowly at first, but eventually the money from the asset box started to fill the income box. After a while, the income box got too full and I had to use that money to buy more assets. Then the money started to replace my physician income, which gave me the freedom to work less, which gave me more time to find more assets to put in the box. It became a self-perpetuating cycle that hasn't stopped.

The process was liberating! After a while, I began to make changes in my orthopedic practice. If there was something I didn't like, I would change it or eliminate it. I could drop insurance companies that didn't pay well. I could hire more people to make my life easier. I didn't need to be on emergency call to provide extra income. If a hospital required me to do something I didn't like, I simply found another place to work that fit my needs. I could travel whenever I wanted without fear of losing income. Since I was generating plenty of income from my asset box, I didn't have to consider the economic impacts of making those changes. I was gaining control.

Suddenly, I started enjoying being a doctor even more. I was able to spend time with my patients and really get to know them because I no longer had to pack the schedule to cover expenses. Then a wonderful thing happened. I looked forward to going to work!

Not only was I having more fun, I had time to explore other passions. I enjoyed real estate, of course, and I was able to devote considerable effort to expanding my knowledge and to producing bigger projects. This led to increased profits and even more free time. I also travelled, learned the guitar, and almost never missed a function for my children. One of the greatest achievements in my life is the fact that my grown children's friends refer to me as the "fun dad," even to this day!

The holy grail of financial freedom is to have all the hallmarks of wealth without depending on active income.

As noted earlier, wealth is not necessarily defined by a number. Many people may *feel* they are rich, claiming large bank accounts and many possessions, but they might not have a healthy work-life balance. Or you might have a good work-life balance but not much money. Even if you have both, if you are trading time every day to keep that lifestyle, you aren't financially free. If you stopped working, all of it would crumble. The holy grail of financial freedom is to have all the hallmarks of wealth without depending on active income.

No matter how you actively make a living, passive income will give you choices and control which you can then use to design the life you want.

Remote Income

One of the beauties of passive income is the ability to own assets that generate money no matter where you are in the world. Remote income can also be produced from anywhere, but it requires some active effort.

I told the story of my friend in Vail who was doing his lawyer work from a mountainside condo. Making money with a computer while staring at the Rockies certainly seemed enticing, and early in my journey I thought that is what I wanted. It was clearly preferable to spending all day in the office or the operating room. But that's not true passive income.

Physicians have told me that they've developed passive income by becoming consultants or providing medical reviews for insurance companies and attorneys. While this is additional income and the work can be done remotely, it's not passive because it still requires active effort to be paid for each task.

A word of caution here: If you choose to expand your active income this way, you'll be tempted to use that money to further enhance your lifestyle. Resist the urge to put this extra profit into your daily checkbook. Otherwise, it will be quickly absorbed by our 21st-century habits of consumerism and immediate gratification, forcing you to count on it every month.

Consider instead putting that extra income into an account dedicated to investing in passive income opportunities. That's essentially what I did. And if you are diligent, that money will grow and give you the means to invest quickly if you see a profitable opportunity. Never underestimate the power of ready cash!

Multiple Streams of Income

There are two schools of thought when it comes to building wealth. One is from industrialist, Andrew Carnegie, who said, "Put all your eggs in one basket and watch that basket." This is a reference to focusing on your core strength and getting the most you can out of it. Think of the obsessions of Steve Jobs, Mark Zuckerberg, and Jeff Bezos. They doggedly worked on one business and each grew their company to staggering proportions. That's a proven way to become rich, but the barrier to entry is high and only a few succeed.

The other side of the coin is reflected in the book *Multiple Streams of Income* by Robert Allen. It describes a strategy of generating income (not all passive) that comes from many different sources. Diversifying your portfolio in this way smooths the ups and downs of fluctuating asset classes and a cycling economy. In the real estate world, for example, you have multiple property options to invest in such as office, retail, multifamily, medical, or industrial. Each reacts differently in different markets. You could even spread these assets out over a large geographic region to protect against local economic downturns.

Multiple streams can also be defined as having your assets in different industries or investment types. You could own real estate, oil properties, dividend-paying stocks, song royalties, or a piece of a business. There are plenty of others to consider, but the point is that with many passive income assets, the intention is that at least some of them will produce income if the others are affected by negative market conditions.

This was evident to me during the dotcom crash in 2001 and the Great Recession in 2008. In each "correction," some of my assets crashed badly, some stayed flat, and some even increased in value. Most importantly, I was comforted in knowing that I wasn't dependent on a single source of income to provide for my family. You will find that the wealthy preserve and grow their assets through multiple streams of income.

Where Do You Find Passive Income?

As discussed earlier, you must get in the game to find passive income opportunities. Start by reading books and blogs to become familiar with who is writing on the subject. Listen to podcasts to hear who is teaching about it. Through these channels, you will discover seminars that will fit your needs. There you will gain knowledge and meet new people. As your network expands, you will meet scores of people who don't "work" for a living and enjoy incomes well above the average for physicians. Through them you will find the right opportunities for you. (To receive information and updates on the world of passive income, visit www.richdoctor.com)

Buckets and Pipelines

We are told to save our way to wealth and retirement, to fill a big bucket with money that we can draw from to finance our lifestyle. How big does that bucket need to be?

One hundred years ago, you were filthy rich if you had a million dollars. Today that's good, but it won't support 25 years of retirement. Inflation will continue to erode your bucket and it will leak. What if the money in the leaky bucket runs out before you do? Nobody has a crystal ball clear enough to determine how much money you will need 25 years from now.

So, unless you become one of the few who creates massive profits from your efforts, you will need something else. That something else is a pipeline of steady income insulated with hard assets that hedge against inflation and produce passive income on a continuous basis. As you grow old, your money will grow with you—and so will your security. Don't carry buckets the rest of your life.

Choices and Control

From a financial perspective, passive income is the most critical concept to internalize, because it's the foundation for creating choices and control, especially for busy professionals.

Most of us have been programmed to make a living by trading time for money. Working hard is a virtue and should never be minimized. But sometimes we get so involved in our careers that we don't see other opportunities in front of us. You can make a million dollars a month, but if it requires the sacrifice of your family, your health, and your dreams, then you will not become a truly rich person, rich in both wealth and spirit. We are given this gift of life only once and I believe we should honor that gift by making the best of it.

Fortunately, you can make your income without sacrificing life's treasures.

The creation of passive income is a liberating and paradigm-shifting process. If you have never experienced it, you can't understand its power.

Close your eyes and imagine walking down the beach in the Maldives. It's on the equator, so it's always sunny. You have just finished diving one of the thousands of coral reefs in the area. You are barefoot. One hand is interlaced with that of your spouse. The other is getting tugged by your child as he or she sees an "awesome shell" every ten feet. Cell service is good and you get an alert on your phone. Although you've been gone for a month, you find out that money has been deposited in your account from one of your passive investments. You're not really sure which one it is, but the money just keeps coming!

What do you do with the money?

You choose!

Create passive income and you create a life of choices and control.

Passive income is additive to your normal income. You can use it to travel, buy your dream car, help a family member, or give it to a worthy cause. If you've not yet reached your desired level of financial freedom, this money can be the seed for your next investment or project.

It becomes a self-perpetuating machine that continually produces more and more income. This begins to generate choices and control in your life. It is then that you will truly understand its power. It is then that you can make the changes that will mold your life into the image you've always dreamed of.

After speaking to far too many doctors who didn't know they could make money without working twelve-hour days, I knew I had to write this chapter to open your eyes to the abundance that is available to you. Expand your means rather than live within your means. Fill the asset box. Build a pipeline. Don't carry buckets. Create passive income and you create a life of choices and control.

PASSIVE INCOME PIPELINE

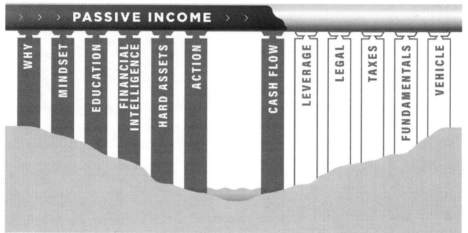

Chapter 10

Cash Flow Is King

Never take your eyes off the cash flow because it's the lifeblood of business.

—Sir Richard Branson, businessman, investor, author

Imagine that you had a bank vault full of gold with a viewing window through which you could see your deposits any time you wanted. It was safely tucked into a secure location and your money was protected. Now imagine that, although all the gold is yours, you don't have the combination for the vault, and it's controlled by someone else. That's what it's like to own assets that don't produce cash flow. On the one hand, it's good to have that pile of gold which represents a portion of your net worth. On the other, if all you can do is look at it, you will still need another source of income to pay for your daily living expenses.

Now imagine you own the vault. Its value is much less than the amount of gold it could contain and your net worth may be less than that of your storage clients. However, you can rent that storage space to as many people as the vault can hold. In fact, the space is big enough to rent to dozens of wealthy gold owners who pay you a monthly fee for your storage services. Those payments provide enough cash flow to cover the costs of running the vault *and* your living expenses.

Net Worth vs. Cash Flow

The two examples above illustrate the difference between net worth and cash flow. Neither one is better than the other. It's best to have a high level of both. But if you can only have one, choose cash flow.

Net worth is the value of all your assets minus the total of all your liabilities. It is a measuring stick that some use to gauge wealth. Some might say they don't need to work harder or become more financially educated because they've developed a large portfolio of stocks, bonds, and mutual funds. They feel their future is secure because they have amassed a large net worth.

However, a high net worth is not the only component of financial independence. If you have a healthy balance sheet, congratulations! That's an important step in the race to become a rich doctor, but in isolation, it won't take you to the finish line.

The secret to being rich is controlling your cash flow. Value that is tied up in non-liquid assets can't be used until released. Don't confuse net worth and cash flow. While it's good to have a high net worth, you also need money to live on. You need cash to make your mortgage payment and to pay the plumber when your toilet backs up. You can't pay for a family trip to Disneyworld with a balance sheet.

The secret to being rich is controlling your cash flow.

As stated in an earlier chapter, you can define wealth as the number of days you can survive without working. A healthy cash flow can make you wealthy for the rest of your life.

If your goal is to buy back time and create freedom and choices in your life, you'll need to cover your basic costs of living. Ideally that comes from passive cash flow. As your cash flow grows, your net worth will naturally grow with it.

So, if you have assets and a strong balance sheet, make sure those assets put real cash in your pocket if you want to accelerate your journey to financial independence.

Cash Flow vs. Capital Gain

In the world of investing and wealth creation, there are two philosophies. One emphasizes the importance of capital gains, the other favors cash flow.

We are all familiar with the adage, "Buy low and sell high." The profit made on the sale is considered a capital gain. Many stock market transactions use the capital gain mechanism. Typically, you buy a share of stock or a mutual fund at a certain price in hopes that it will rise over time. When you sell, the difference between the purchase and the sales price is your capital gain.

The same mechanism can be used in the real estate world. You can buy a property at a relatively low price, improve the structure, the appearance, or the occupancy rate, and sell it for a higher price. Again, the difference between the purchase and sales price is your profit, or capital gain.

The examples above produce a one-time payment for value received. In each, a sale is required to capture the profit. As a physician or professional, our capital gain occurs only after we invest time to provide our service. It's called a salary.

The second method of wealth creation is the school of cash flow. In this system, the entrepreneur provides a product or service to a customer, or invests capital, in return for regular cash flow. Depending on the product, service or investment, this payment can go on for years or even decades. The primary effort is produced once but the payment continues, with minimal additional effort.

You can define wealth as the number of days you can survive without working.

Consider your phone bill. While you may have purchased your Apple or Android phone, it does you no good without the monthly phone and data service. The service companies invest in towers and infrastructure that can handle multiple subscribers. This cash flow comes into those companies regularly, on a monthly basis. The revenue increases as the subscriber base grows but most of the effort has already taken place.

The product stays the same, whether they serve one person or a million. Obviously a million subscribers will provide higher cash flow!

In the real estate world, entrepreneurs buy or build property and then make that property available to tenants to rent. This monthly rent provides cash flow. In the paper market, some companies provide cash flow in the form of regular stock dividends. You can loan money and collect regular principal and interest payments. These are just a few of the many ways to produce cash flow.

We've all heard the saying "cash is king." In the world of financial freedom, cash flow is king. It is the building block of passive income which is the key to financial freedom.

Is Capital Gain Bad?

There is nothing wrong with a large capital gain. If it's big enough, you might be able to live off it for the rest of your life. I wish I had the talent of a Jeff Bezos or other successful entrepreneurs who hit the jackpot with their companies, but that didn't fit my training or psychology. Generating cash flow through multiple investments did. After all, with a cash flow mindset, you don't have to become a billionaire. You just need to produce enough to pay for your living expenses. Once that's accomplished, you will be financially free.

I love the occasional capital gain and have celebrated many of them—most recently from a property refinance. I felt wealthy, so I went shopping. However, I didn't go to the Ferrari dealership. I went to the asset store! I did keep some for fun but used most of it to create more monthly income that will keep flowing for years to come. And that, you'll recall, is the point of cash flow: to replace your working income so that you will be free to pursue any course in life you choose.

One issue with capital gains is that after you produce one, you must begin the process again to create another. Consider a real estate example. In most markets, you can buy a single-family home in need of repair for a reasonable price. After hiring contractors or doing the work yourself, you can usually sell it for a profit. Happy days! Time to celebrate and use the money as you see fit. Once the celebration is over, though, if you want to feel that same euphoria, you must repeat the process. Many people have used this formula successfully, but if you are a physician, odds are that you won't have the time or resources to do this on a regular basis.

Consider a second example with the same house. You buy it, renovate it, and then, instead of selling it, you rent it. Furthermore, you hire a manager who takes care of all the details and sends you a check every month. This becomes a cash flow machine that works twenty-four hours a day whether you are sleeping, working, or vacationing.

Both methods of investment have their pros and cons. Capital gains investing returns your principal back faster but requires repeated effort. Cash flow investing requires time to get back principal, but the bulk of the effort is expended only once. I am not saying one is better for you than the other. That's for you to decide. For me, I chose to focus on cash flow.

As a physician, I already had a good source of monthly income from my job and decided to use some of it to start creating small streams of passive income. I repeated that process with many different assets and eventually those small payments started to multiply. It was slow at first and not a life-changer. However, those monthly payments began to add up. And after a while, I was able to accelerate the process and buy larger and larger properties. Over time, the monthly cash flow from those investments eclipsed my orthopedic monthly income.

It was then that I became financially free.

Weathering the Storms

In the world of finance and investing, there are always seasons. Sometimes it's bright and cheerful, like summer. The economy is healthy and everybody seems to be making money. Inevitably, winter comes and the economy softens. People lose jobs and the climate becomes gloomy. The airwaves fill with experts talking about how bad everything is: jobs, the stock market, manufacturing, real estate values. People feel less wealthy because their stock portfolios decline and they don't have as much equity in their homes.

How does that affect a cash flow investor? Let's consider a real estate example again. It is often during these times that people will say that real estate is a bad investment. Home values decline, foreclosures increase, and home builder stocks decline. The media proclaims that real estate is dead as a viable investment. This is probably true if you rely on selling the property for more than what you bought it for.

A cash flow investor will be less concerned. Cash flow investors do not require values to increase to make their profit. They buy based on the cash flow that an asset can produce.

Assume you purchased an asset for $10 million and it provides free cash flow of $100,000/year after all expenses are paid, including the mortgage. If the economy slips and your property is now worth $8 million but still produces $100,000 in cash flow, are you that much worse off? If things go really bad and cash flow decreases, you'll still make some profit and you keep your property. Even if cash flow goes to zero, if your rent still covers expenses, your tenants are paying down the loan and you are still getting ahead.

The above example is simplified and assumes you have enough rent to cover each scenario. Real estate can become cash flow negative, but it is your education that will help you avoid that situation. While there are no fail-safe methods to protect against Armageddon, if you invest for cash flow, you will more easily be able to weather the storm. If you must sell to make your profit or to recover your investment, this scenario will be painful.

Whatever vehicle(s) you choose, if the cash flow replaces your living expenses, you are free.

And, as I have emphasized throughout this book, one of the most common vehicles available to us as professionals is real estate. Most physicians have some degree of discretionary income to invest which can be placed into real estate in a passive manner that requires no time from an already busy schedule. You provide funds for the project and the other partners do all the work. If things go right, you'll receive regular income based on the performance of the investment.

Remember, your goal is to create cash flow that you don't have to work for. Whatever vehicle(s) you choose, if the cash flow replaces your living expenses, you're free. Then you can choose what you would like to do next.

Define Your Expenses

If you are going to replace your expenses, it's important to know exactly what those numbers are. You could probably make a rough estimate off the top of your head, but with inaccurate numbers, you'll tend to miss hidden amounts which will produce inaccurate results. This is where you must be honest with yourself. If you wish to create productive change, you must acknowledge all of your expenses or you won't be able to efficiently move forward with your goal. So write down *everything* you spend.

I did this early, when I was just out of medical training. Luckily, my wife liked to budget and she knew what we spent on the big items. Later, we used software programs that could produce income and expense reports. Using my wife's budget and the numbers from the reports, we were able to categorize most of our outlays. A pleasant side effect of knowing what you spend is that you will typically end up spending less, which frees up more income to be used for cash-flowing investments.

We kept track of the main expenses, including the house payment, car payments, groceries, outside meals, utilities, children's school and activities, property taxes, income taxes, healthcare and travel. Those categories gave me the first numbers to shoot for.

For me, the easiest way to track these payments was to use a software program such as Quicken or QuickBooks. Every year, with the push of a few buttons, I could see every expense divided into neat categories. That gave me the opportunity to evaluate where we were spending our money. If there were drastic differences from year to year, I could make changes.

▶ ACTION ITEM ◀

Purchase software, create categories for everything you spend, then track your expenses.

As my journey to passive income progressed, I would play a game and decide which category I had replaced. After a while, I could say I had covered my utilities, then groceries, then taxes, and so on. It was new and exciting and I was making progress. That approach also eliminated the heavy weight of trying to become financially free in one big move. It relaxed me.

During this process I did pay off my house and the cars, although there are valid arguments for keeping those two items on a payment plan. With the low cost of home and car loans, that money could have been used for investments that would have increased my passive cash flow. So I'm not perfect. My emotional make-up wanted to eliminate those costs because those "assets" didn't produce income for me. If something didn't put money in my pocket, I didn't want to carry the debt on it. In my mind, that was "bad debt," which will be discussed in a later chapter.

It took a while, but eventually I covered all my expenses with enough cash flow to support my basic lifestyle and some travel. I had finally replaced the need for my working income.

Pause here and let that last sentence sink in.

Financially, I no longer had to work. I was liberated. I now had ultimate control over what I did for the rest of my life. How would that feel to you? Let your mind wander and think about what you could do for yourself, your family, and the world. You could enjoy medicine for the very reasons that drew you to become a doctor. You could learn a new language, do research, travel the world, staff unfunded medical clinics, write a book, start a business or take acting lessons. The options are endless!

That's the freedom of replacing your expenses through passive cash flow. It's a great feeling and opens doors you didn't know existed. It has felt so good to me that it's one of the big reasons I wanted to share it with you in this book.

Beware of the Consumer Trap

I wish I could tell you that I did all of that perfectly and without any mistakes. *Au contraire.*

Remember when I said that I categorized my expenses soon after I got out of training? I was still living like a student and my costs were low. I determined that I was living off about 30 percent of my salary. I had money to burn and I assumed it would only get better from there. Big mistake!

I had two cars that were both paid off, the same ones my wife and I drove during my training. Our first house was nice but not too expensive. Our kids had not started their journey into every paid activity possible and we hadn't fully entered the "social scene." I had not yet been indoctrinated into the world of the successful professional.

Fast forward a few years. My income had more than doubled but I was now living off close to 100 percent of that new number. Yikes!

The cost of the "professional" lifestyle is like a thief in the night. It creeps in when you are sleeping and steals things you sometimes don't notice for a while. All of a sudden, you realize you are paying a month's salary for karate lessons, dance lessons, and tutoring. Another month goes to a nicer car that "fits" the profile of a physician or his wife. Of course, you need a bigger house in the best neighborhood, so that takes the rest.

At some point, I noticed that my journey to financial freedom was spinning in the mud, so I eliminated some frivolous costs and doubled down on my cash flow efforts. I tell you this not to keep your kids out of karate or dance, or to suggest that you live like a hermit. Just be aware of the potential "expense creep". A small amount of awareness early can lead to a life of abundance later.

Again, my goal is not for you to live within your means but to expand your means so you can live the life of your dreams.

The Velocity of Money

As you develop cash flow, there will come a point at which you will have covered all your expenses. Then what do you do? You can't just let that cash sit around. Inflation attacks idle cash and money will lose value if it doesn't stay in motion.

This is the concept of the velocity of money. As you gain some financial freedom, utilize what you've learned to keep your money moving. Money is a fabulous employee and it will gladly work around the clock. The higher the velocity of your money, the faster it grows and the sooner you'll reach your goals.

While it's good to have cash readily available to handle emergencies or take quick advantage of investment opportunities, idle cash does not make you money. At a minimum, put those accessible funds into something whose value will keep up with inflation. This will keep your cash position safe as it continues to grow your wealth.

Money is a fabulous employee and it will gladly work around the clock.

As noted earlier, when I receive a large sum of money for any reason, I shop for investments that produce cash flow or preserve my capital in the face of inflation. This can involve gold, insurance, government debt, or certain types of real estate. I will discuss some of these in later chapters but consult your advisors for what is right for you.

Chasing Home Runs

Over my nearly three decades as a practicing physician, I've been amazed at what doctors invest in. Many are attracted to start-up ventures that sound sexy and have unreasonable expectations of huge profits. To use a baseball metaphor, these doctors are swinging for the fences. Such home runs are exciting but rare.

Some of my colleagues are attracted to projects that primarily promise capital gains. Cash flow doesn't seem to excite them. I don't understand their thinking. Perhaps it's because they already have good salaries and can't imagine replacing it with something as simple and incremental as passive income. Passive cash flow can come off as boring. It's certainly not as sexy as a big windfall.

I never wanted to get out of medicine. I just wanted enough passive cash flow to cover my bills. In baseball terms, I was hitting for singles rather than home runs. I was looking for small victories. I was intrigued by not having to do a unit of work for a unit of pay. "Mailbox money" was exciting to me and something I didn't possess. I wasn't looking to escape a cubicle; I just wanted to have more choices in life.

And it worked. I won the game with a series of singles and the occasional double. All my essential needs are covered by regular cash flow. Now I can swing for the fences if I want to because it won't negatively affect my lifestyle.

My goal is to make cash flow look sexy to you. I realize that beauty is in the eye of the beholder and hope I've opened your eyes to the magnificence of free cash flow. It can't buy you love or happiness, but it might give you the time to find them!

As you begin your journey to financial freedom, consider making cash flow a priority. Eliminating reliance on your working income will give you the freedom to choose your next move. Cash flow has given me the latitude to pursue my passions and my mission: to free doctors financially so we can have a caring and humane healthcare system with happy physicians. There is no retirement for me. There is only mission. Join me.

BUILDING YOUR
PASSIVE INCOME PIPELINE

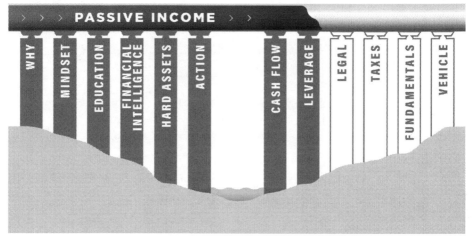

Chapter 11

The Magic of Leverage

Rich people use debt to leverage investments and grow cash flows. Poor people use debt to buy things that make rich people richer.

—GRANT CARDONE

The Great Pyramid of Giza took 20 years to build. It's 479 feet high and covers an area the size of two football fields. It was built sometime between 2589 BC and 2566 BC during the reign of Khufu of the 4th Dynasty. The average weight of each building block was 2.5 tons and the stones were meticulously moved into place with long iron poles to less than eight inches apart.[47, 48]

A single man can move a 30-ton shipping container by manipulating a few hand controls on a crane.

A doctor can control a $40 million apartment building with only $100,000 of his or her own money.

What do these three actions have in common? Each is an example of the use of leverage.

Archimedes first described leverage in the third century BC when he stated that force could be amplified with the use of a lever. More broadly, leverage is the concept of accomplishing more with the same or less effort. According to BusinessDictionary.com, "Leverage is the ability to influence a system, or an environment, in a way that multiplies the outcome of one's efforts without a corresponding increase in the consumption of resources."

While leverage can be used to magnify physical results, it can also be applied to many other areas of life. It is one way in which extraordinary things are accomplished that at first seemed impossible.

If you're seeking financial independence, especially if you are a busy doctor, you will need leverage to accomplish your goal. Many types of leverage can be used to multiply your efforts. If you use them wisely, you will build your passive income pipeline faster.

Financial Leverage

If passive income is the key to financial freedom, and cash flow is the building block of passive income, then financial leverage is the instrument to achieve both faster and better.

What is financial leverage?

If you have ever purchased a house, a car, or your education by obtaining a loan, you have used financial leverage. This is debt and is sometimes referred to as the use of "other people's money" or OPM. Financial leverage is an important tool in your journey to financial independence because it allows you to control large sums of money with only small amounts of your own.

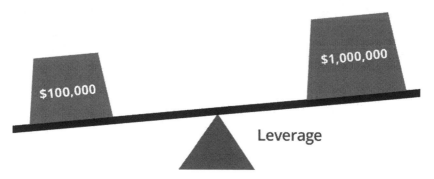

Debt increases the velocity of your money because you don't have to use all your own capital for every investment or project. It allows you to participate in more investments, do more deals, or buy something bigger than you could without a loan. Remember, as discussed in the last chapter, if you increase the velocity of your money, you obtain more rather than less, and sooner rather than later. This accelerates your path to financial independence.

Most of us have been taught that debt is bad. In fact, this advice goes back centuries. In Shakespeare's *Hamlet*, Polonius entreats Laertes to "Neither a borrower nor lender be." Benjamin Franklin is quoted as saying, "Rather go to bed without dinner than to rise in debt." More recently, radio host and financial author Dave Ramsey contended that, "You can't be in debt and win. It doesn't work."

It's no wonder everybody is scared of debt. For the average person who is up to his ears in consumer debt, this is sound advice. If you don't understand how money works and aren't financially educated, debt can swallow your life and you should avoid it. However, if you understand how to properly use it, debt can set you free. Rich people use debt as a tool to create more wealth.

The proper use of financial leverage depends on the type of debt you are using. There are two kinds: bad debt and good debt.

Bad Debt

Bad debt buys products and services that don't put money in your pocket and must be repaid from your personal income. This is the type of debt referred to above by Shakespeare, Franklin, and Ramsey.

Unfortunately, these loans are part of the fabric of modern life. We borrow for such things as cars, houses, furniture, school, phones, and vacations. Credit cards are available to almost anyone and make it easy to live on bad debt. Outsized personal debt levels have become epidemic and validate why we often see admonitions to avoid using credit to live beyond our means. That's the type of debt to avoid. A poor doctor uses bad debt.

Bad debt buys products and services that don't put money in your pocket and must be repaid from your personal income.

As physicians, we command enviable incomes, which attract banks and lenders of all sorts. It's intoxicating to know that with the stroke of a pen, you can have a bundle of money at your disposal to use as you wish. Resist the temptation! If you can afford a Chevy but need a bigger loan to buy a Tesla, buy the Chevy. Neither one will put money in your pocket and neither is an asset.

In this context, you should do whatever you can to avoid debt. Neither your fancy car nor your new furniture will ever produce income for you. They will continue to lose value and the debt will remain until you pay it off.

Good Debt

On the other hand, there is "good debt." Good debt buys a productive asset that puts money in your pocket *and* is paid by someone else. Rich doctors use good debt. Why would somebody else pay your debts? Read on!

Consider a simple comparison. When buying a house, most people require a personal loan from the bank. You pay 10-20 percent of the purchase price and the bank gives you a mortgage for the remaining 80-90 percent. You are responsible for the loan and pay it out of available funds from your paycheck. That loan remains in place and is your responsibility until it is fully paid off. This is how most people purchase their homes.

If you are an investor, you might buy the same house. You put 20-25 percent down and the bank gives you the rest as a *commercial* loan. Instead of living in the house, you rent it to a nice couple from California. It's close to their children's school and they love the back yard. Their rent payment covers your operating expenses and the monthly mortgage payment. They direct-deposit a check to your account every month without fail.

Good debt buys a productive asset that puts money in your pocket and is paid by someone else.

These folks are paying your mortgage and they are more than happy to do it. You have provided them with a good clean house, in a neighborhood they like, and it's within their budget. Their rent payment covers your debt and puts money in your pocket. Both parties win. This is good debt.

Good debt offers the kind of leverage that will accelerate your path to financial independence. You can own more assets and produce more wealth by using OPM. While this may sound odd to you now, the people who have the money *want* to lend it to you. Banks make their money by lending their deposits to others for higher interest rates. Investors will lend to you because they want their money to grow.

Financial leverage, in the form of debt, can be used to buy real estate, businesses, stocks, and many other income-producing vehicles. Be aware, though, that this can be a double-edged sword. Leverage is great when your asset is productive, but it can accelerate your losses if you have a bad asset. This is why your financial education is so important. It's your defense against purchasing a bad asset.

Financial leverage, in the form of good debt, is a powerful tool that, if wisely used, can accelerate your journey to financial freedom. In fact, it's very difficult to build a large passive income portfolio without it.

Time Leverage

Let's face it, as doctors, time is the one thing that we don't have. That's why the ability to leverage time is crucial if you want to become a rich doctor.

Think about the time you spend doing things that don't make you money, such as EMR inputting, staff meetings and returning phone calls. These are all seemingly necessary parts of your professional life, but are they the best use of your time and are they helping you get to your goal of financial freedom? What if you could eliminate those unproductive responsibilities with the use of leverage?

The ability to leverage time is crucial if you want to become a rich doctor.

You can do this by hiring employees to do the jobs that don't require your professional level of training such as office staff and physician extenders. Ultimately, if perfectly leveraged, you will only perform tasks that produce the maximum output. But this requires more than just hiring people.

You must develop a mindset of time efficiency. Delegate tasks that can be done by others. Prioritize what is and isn't important (or what makes you money and what doesn't). Set goals and then determine the activities that will help you reach them the fastest. Eliminate those that are extra weight. Hire to your weaknesses and develop your strengths to leverage your time to the fullest.

We all have the same number of hours in a day. The difference between the rich and the poor is how they use that time. You could have chosen to watch television or read a spy novel but instead you are reading a book about wealth and mindset. Such use of your time will make you a rich doctor!

Knowledge Leverage

Nobody can know everything. Not even a doctor!

We constantly leverage the knowledge of others to succeed in life. Around the house, I can fix some plumbing and perform basic carpentry because of my training as an orthopedic surgeon, but I won't touch electricity. I call the expert. Likewise, though I have a good working knowledge of some real estate law, my company always hires top real estate attorneys for our projects.

> ## ▶ ACTION ITEM ◀
> List the things that require your time that can be done by others. Can you hire someone to do these tasks?

Automobile tycoon, Henry Ford was once grilled by an attorney during a trial reportedly to demonstrate that he was ignorant. During the process, it was apparent that he didn't know many of the answers to the questions being asked. Finally, exasperated and tired, Ford said, "Tell me why I should clutter up my mind with general knowledge, for the purpose of being able to answer questions, when I have men around me who can supply any knowledge I require?"[49]

Henry Ford knew how to leverage the knowledge of others and look where it got him!

I couldn't function or flourish without the wonderful people that surround me. I've had two real estate partners who have helped me make a lot of money. I have brilliant lawyers, CPA's, developers, contractors, managers, and physician assistants. They all have expertise in their fields, as I have in mine. We leverage each other to make all our lives better; in some cases, we make the lives of others better with our work.

Experience Leverage

There's an old saying in the real estate world that to make a deal, at least two people must come together. Typically, one has the money and the other has the experience. When the deal is complete, the roles have reversed!

Ouch!

I only say that because I've been a part of that equation and it hurts. Subsequently, I made a rule that I would always listen to my mentors or people with more experience. If I couldn't convince them that something was a good deal, even if I disagreed, I would not invest. That rule has worked well for me.

Unfortunately, it took me a few years to realize that it's better to leverage the experience of others. Up until then, most of my missteps had been my own and I paid for them personally. Experience usually comes from mistakes, so I finally figured it would be much less painful if I could learn from other people's mistakes instead of mine.

Fortunately, there are people out there who have been where you want to go and many would be happy to guide you there. Seek out mentors and respect their experience. They only want you to succeed. Use the leverage that they willingly give you. Pay for their guidance if you must. The cost will be minuscule compared to the losses you may incur without it. These mentors could be partners, deal sponsors, or paid coaches. I have a business coach who has saved me tremendous heartache, and some of the most successful people I know still have coaches. It pays to listen.

Relationship Leverage

My insurance agent says that many of his clients are found on the golf course. I believe him because I have played golf with him and he has provided my insurance for 28 years. Am I the victim of a slick sales technique? Not in my mind. He's just a good friend who happens to be my insurance agent. I know he needs to make a living and I believe he truly has my best interests in mind.

That's one way to leverage a relationship. People like to do business with folks they know, like, and trust. Some of the biggest deals in the world have been done between people who already had a previous relationship.

When my son was five years old, he became friends with one of his soccer teammates. My wife and I then became friends with his parents. That led to meeting some of their friends who all worked together at a small start-up tech company. I was a physician and had no clue what they did, even after they explained it to me. It didn't matter; we just enjoyed hanging out together.

About a year later, the boy's father called up and asked if I would like to be included in "Friends and Family" for his company's initial public offering. I didn't yet know that process, so he explained it and I gladly accepted. I was handsomely rewarded when their company went public within the next six months.

The point of the story is that my wife and I had made friends. We had no idea what their company did, or what position the father held, because that is not how we judge friendship. We got along great, built a relationship and developed trust. Our profit was an offshoot of a genuine relationship, not part of a plan.

Another way to benefit from your relationships is through their connections to others. People always feel more comfortable when they meet someone who has been referred by a friend. Think about patients who have been referred by friends or a trusted physician. It's like a second date or a follow-up job interview. A certain level of trust has already been established. It helps you move faster and more efficiently. Being connected to others is a form of leverage.

Do your best to help others succeed and you will be rewarded.

Become a connector yourself and you will be connected. Introduce your friends to your circle of influence. Someone you know may have the answer to someone else's problem. Do your best to help others succeed and you will be rewarded.

Personally, I think the relationship part of life and business is the fun part. Even if no deal is ever struck, you will have made a new friend.

Technology Leverage

As a busy professional, technology has made it easier to have outside interests and stay on top of them. I can use my phone to keep up with my personal properties and stay in touch with my real estate office from anywhere in the world. Recently I was in Kazakhstan and there was barely a break in communication. When necessary, I schedule physical meetings from the phone. If you are a passive investor, you can keep track of everything remotely through technology.

Social media can be used to connect with like-minded groups where everyone can leverage the collective knowledge base of the group. There are podcasts for virtually every subject you might be interested in. Video meetings with screen shares can be arranged for free. Clients, investors, and joint venture partners can all see the same information in real-time and be anywhere in the world. Investors can leverage crowdfunding sites and become privy to opportunities they might have otherwise never seen. These are examples of efficient ways to leverage technology for education, connection, and operation.

In the real estate world, technology has made it easier to distribute tax statements and cash distributions with the push of a button. If you're an investor in one of our projects, the quarterly distribution just shows up in your bank account at the appropriate time. We use drones to take videos or photos of our apartment developments to show to investors.

Technology improves rapidly and will likely always play a role in your future investments.

Teamwork

The most successful business owners and investors spend a great deal of time and money forming teams to reach their goals. That's because teamwork combines multiple forms of leverage and is an important component in the quest for financial freedom. Extraordinary results are achieved by teams. Behind most successful individuals is a functioning team with diverse talents. Steve Jobs didn't build Apple alone and Neil Armstrong didn't walk on the moon without the help of a talented team.

The 2013 movie *The Internship*, starring Owen Wilson and Vince Vaughn, is about two recently laid-off salesmen who apply for an internship at Google. They use their sales skills to fake their way in, but it quickly becomes apparent that they are way out of their league in the digital environment. The intern program is populated with tech-savvy millennials from Harvard, Stanford, and the rest of the "best" schools. A team contest is created for the interns to compete for a real job at Google. The interns from the good schools band together while the two "dinosaurs" are left on a team comprised of the rejects.

As the competition progresses, it is painfully and humorously evident that these two older guys just don't have tech skills. However, they do have sales and teamwork skills. Eventually, they form a cohesive team out of the misfit intern candidates. They win the competition and their team is awarded the job. The lead recruiter tells them that it was their ability to work as a team, not their individual attributes, that set them apart from the competition.

The most successful business owners and investors spend a great deal of time and money forming teams to reach their goals.

We all need a team. When I started my practice, I was convinced that only I could do a job correctly. This is where I had to embrace a paradigm shift and realize that I did not have all the answers. I had to learn to leverage the capabilities of others. It turned out to be a game-changer. I learned valuable lessons and my success was multiplied many times over.

While being a member of a team can be exhilarating, it can also be painful. It takes hard work to be a productive part of a high-functioning team. To have a well-oiled machine that churns out income, everyone must do their job and learn how to work together. Sometimes it requires compromise and usually requires that you leave your ego at the door. As doctors, we are used to having the final word on everything. It takes a lot of emotional maturity to submit to the team mission rather than your own desires. But the rewards can be staggering.

You can make more money and achieve your goals sooner, without doing all the work yourself, if you create teams. It's also an awesome way to create financial independence while you are still working as a doctor.

Creating Your Team

Once you've escaped the mindset of "only I can do this job", you will need to form a team. The first recruit should be your spouse. He or she can be your most important collaborator. Nothing is more powerful than a couple with the same goals. If your spouse isn't in sync with your goals or the idea of passive income, you can still climb the mountain, but the path might be rockier.

While I have a portfolio of individually owned companies and real estate, my greatest successes have come from working with business partners. My first partner started as a friend and became a mentor. My second partner started as a stranger, became a friend, and is my current business partner. My successes have been tangibly multiplied by knowing and working with these two men.

Unfortunately, these are not the only partners I've had. Between those lines are tales of bad partners and mistakes made. It's been a journey, but the lessons learned were priceless and they led to eventual success. Needless to say, choose your partners wisely. A bad partner can cause you grief, but a good partner is worth his or her weight in gold.

In addition to partners and spouses, you will ultimately need bookkeepers, lawyers, CPA's, bankers, brokers, tech advisors, and possibly tradespeople. If you don't know how or where to find these team members, use your network of relationships to ask successful entrepreneurs who they use. Over time, you'll construct your "financial freedom team." (For updated resources to help you create your team, visit www.richdoctor.com/tools)

As a busy doctor, you might be reading this and saying, "I don't have time to put a team together. My work and family take up most of my time." Fear not. You can continue to live your life while taking advantage of a team that is already in place with the use of *syndication*.

Syndication

Syndication is a tool that deserves special mention here. It's another form of leverage that works for two or more parties at the same time. It is a perfect tool for the busy doctor.

In the world of investment, there are two basic groups of people: Those with knowledge and experience who put in the sweat equity to construct solid investment projects, and those who don't have that expertise but have funds they want to put to work.

Syndication is a viable way for busy doctors to enjoy the benefits of investing without taking time away from their work.

The process of syndication brings these two parties together. It's another form of leverage. The group or individual who puts the investment together is often called the Sponsor. When funds are required for a project, they make the investment available to investors. This helps both parties. On the sponsor side, they do all the work but use other people's money to fund the project. On the investor side, they do no work but can utilize the expertise of the sponsor to create a return on their money.

This is a viable way for busy doctors to enjoy the benefits of investing without taking time away from their work. I know many professionals who have amassed large investment portfolios by participating passively in the syndication model. You don't have to do the work yourself. You leverage the skills of others to create financial freedom.

Leverage is a tool for accelerating your journey to financial independence. Use it wisely and like magic, it will set you free!

BUILDING YOUR
PASSIVE INCOME PIPELINE

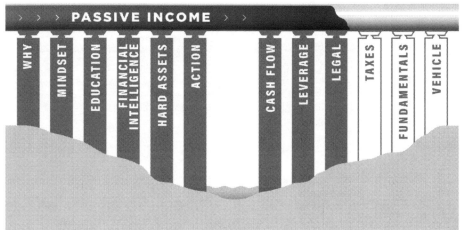

Chapter 12

Protect Your Stuff

Where there is a will, there is a lawsuit.

—ADDISON MIZNER, AMERICAN ARCHITECT

I was once involved in a lawsuit and was sitting across from an attorney who apparently had watched too many legal shows on TV. It was all going to work out but had progressed to the deposition stage. I was there with my real estate partner. We owned a large office complex and there was disagreement with the neighbor about who had access to the gate between the two properties. It was a minor dispute.

I was in a good mood, but the opposing attorney started with a flourish and a series of questions related to medicine and malpractice suits presumably designed to decrease my credibility. I had no problem discussing this subject, but I failed to see the connection between medicine and a disagreement about a gate.

At one point, he asked me if I owned the office complex. By then I was in a playful but non-cooperative mood, so I said "No." He asked if I was a partner in the partnership that owned the complex. I said "No." He was perplexed, took a break, and then came back ten minutes later. He asked if I was a partner in a limited partnership that owned an interest in the office complex. The answer to that was, "Yes."

Why did I present that example?

Although I was there to answer questions about the lawsuit, I had no personal ownership of the real estate. I obtained my financial interest through a limited partnership, which is a separate entity from me. I was playing with the guy, but I could legally state that I personally had no ownership of the office complex. As I learned in an asset protection seminar, a limited liability partnership has a separate soul from me and is a completely different entity.

This is an important concept if you want to protect what is yours.

Separate Your Assets

Years ago, I read a book called *Cover Your Assets* by Jay Mitton. In addition to the catchy title, I liked the book because it started me on a path of asset protection before I had much to lose. I figured it was better to start early and shield my assets before I found out that they needed protection.

As a physician, it's prudent to separate your assets from your everyday medical life. As you morph into an experienced, cash flow-producing machine, you don't want to expose your passive income-producing holdings to predatory patients and lawyers. It's no secret that the medical field has its share of litigation. Most of the time, a loss is covered by malpractice insurance, but sometimes it's not and your personal property can be at risk. If your investment assets aren't separated from your personal assets, they could be lost.

If your investment assets aren't separated from your personal assets, they could be lost.

Your medical practice is not the only place that will expose your assets to risk. Outside of medicine there are plenty of other predators. You might be involved in a car accident and cause harm to another person. Someone could injure themselves at one of your properties or at your business. If a plaintiff sues and prevails, your personal wealth can be attacked.

Let's assume you are mid-way through your journey to financial freedom. You own real estate, paper assets, commodities, businesses, and precious metals. Do you want those assets to be vulnerable in today's litigious society? Of course not.

If you've built your team wisely, you will have an attorney who can structure the ownership of your holdings in such a manner that they will be protected from those who would wish to take them away from you. Typically, your attorney will form separate companies to hold different assets.

The time to create these companies is when your investments are small. Then, your wealth can grow inside the protection of a properly designed legal vehicle. These entities must also be set up before you are involved in any type of litigation. Once a lawsuit starts, you can't move your assets.

I received this advice early in my career and it stuck. Almost all my assets are owned by separate entities and are not in my personal name. In my real estate company, we create separate entities for each individual investment. This limits the investors' and the property's exposure to outside liability. Everything is packaged into neat bundles to stop the spread of liability to other valuable assets. It's like an isolation chamber for a contagious disease. It helps to prevent a legal epidemic!

While these structures can't prevent lawsuits and don't take the place of proper insurance, knowing that my assets are as protected as legally possible gives me some peace of mind.

Limit Your Losses

There are many options for structuring the ownership of investment assets. At the end of this chapter, my friend and legal expert, Garrett Sutton, will provide a brief overview of them. For now, it's important to realize that there are primarily two types of investment vehicles that will concern you as a new rich doctor: those you create to protect your personal assets, and those created by others for you to invest in their projects.

When you are investing with other people, these deals will typically be structured either as Limited Liability Companies (LLCs) or Limited Partnerships (LPs), but the mechanics will be very similar. The key thing to know about both is that they help to mitigate risk and limit your losses. Not only do they separate your assets so they can't all be lost at once; they limit the amount of money you can lose.

If you invest in a limited liability structure, you are only putting the amount of your original investment at risk.

This is an important point to understand regarding asset protection. Nobody wants to lose any of their money, but it's an unfortunate fact that not every investment works. If you invest in a limited liability structure, you are only putting the amount of your original investment at risk. The legal structure allows for protection against further losses. This gives you the security of knowing that if a catastrophe occurs, your losses are limited to the amount that you put into the project. Thus, it will not affect resources that you might have earmarked for the next investment. Professional investors always try to limit their losses.

For my personal investments, LPs and LLCs have served me well in compartmentalizing my assets. Separation is important because, as noted before, it's a litigious society and people love to get stuff for free. If someone falls on your front porch and finds out you are worth millions of dollars, they're going to try to get some for themselves.

These entities serve to deter those types of attacks. That's why I told the story at the beginning of the chapter. Personally, I owned none of the real estate in question. So, if somebody falls on my porch, they can't get any money from the medical real estate. It's owned by another company, but I have control of that company.

Own Nothing but Control Everything

In our lawsuit-crazy society, the best protection is to own nothing and control everything. The more you can separate your assets, the safer you will be. There are limits to this and the complexity goes up as you add entities. The choice you make will depend on your appetite for protection versus simplicity. The more separated and protected you are, the higher the complexity and the cost. However, there's a comfortable middle ground for everyone.

> *In our lawsuit-crazy society, the best protection is to own*
> *nothing and control everything.*

My strategy has been to create separate entities that own different types of assets. One has tenants and carries more risk. That partnership has a generous liability and property insurance policy in place. If someone does injure themselves at one of my properties, the assets within that partnership could be attacked by a plaintiff. Of course, liability would still need to be proven and the amount of loss would have to eclipse the insurance policy. However, a problem in this partnership will not carry over to other assets that are owned by completely different companies.

Another one of my partnerships only buys limited liability shares in other projects. Those could be my own projects or a deal that someone else has put together. There is no liability within this partnership. Externally, it would be very difficult for someone to get to the assets inside that partnership because it's a separately owned company that has nothing to do with my other assets. Internally there is no risk, meaning that no lawsuits will come from within the partnership because it performs no services that could trigger a lawsuit. It only owns limited liability shares, not the actual property.

I use a third partnership for speculative investments; it has its own source of cash flow and is a way to separate "riskier" speculation from my stable cash-flowing partnerships.

Even if someone did prevail in a personal lawsuit, they would have great difficulty getting to my ownership of these partnerships. The Internal Revenue Service recognizes each entity as a separate being, as I was told 25 years ago in that asset protection seminar. They each have different tax identification numbers and bank accounts. Each company files a separate tax return. If one company gets sued, the others are not affected.

Let's put this inside a medical scenario. You are in a group of five doctors. One of them commits a horrible act of malpractice. If your assets aren't properly separated from him, you could be forced to pay for the claim against him. Without proper asset protection, you could have the financial equivalent of taking responsibility for another doctor's medical malpractice!

While it's a hassle to have multiple entities for your investment program, the feeling of security they provide might be worth the effort. It only takes one lawsuit to support the value of separating your assets. If you think you can't or don't want to spend the time creating and managing them, there are companies that can help. I still do it myself and it takes less than one hour per month. A small price to pay for peace of mind.

Legal Documents

If you start on the path to financial freedom and become an investor, you will be well-advised to have an attorney guide you through the paperwork. As noted above, most investments are structured into some sort of limited liability vehicle. If you are a passive investor, you'll be presented with legal paperwork describing everything there is to know about the investment. That paperwork is also designed to prove that the sponsor has disclosed everything about the opportunity. You will be expected to read and sign these documents.

When I speak to doctors across the country, I frequently receive questions about the legal mechanics of investing. I'm not a lawyer and don't give legal advice, but I can provide a basic primer on legal basics from the investor's point of view.

SUBSCRIPTION AGREEMENT

If you invest in someone else's project, you'll first receive what is called a Subscription Agreement. It proves to the sponsor that you're legally able to participate in the project and have sufficient resources to make the investment. It also documents that you have enough financial stability to withstand the unlikely loss of your money. Don't let that scare you. Typically, the sponsors have their own money at risk. They will do everything in their power to make it a successful investment.

PRIVATE PLACEMENT MEMORANDUM

Next is the Private Placement Memorandum. This document is designed to give you all the information you need about the investment, including how it's structured, it's projected returns, and its risks. The first time most people read one of these they freak out because every possible risk is listed, from natural disasters to a bad business plan. When you sign it, you acknowledge that you understand you can lose all your money. However, as you read further in the document, you will see that the investment is projected to be successful.

COMPANY AGREEMENT

Finally, you'll receive the Company Agreement, also known as an Operating Agreement, which outlines the structure and function of the company. Typically, this company (partnership) has been set up for the sole purpose of owning this one single asset (more liability protection.) The Company Agreement will outline the leadership of the company and will give the details of how it will function. You'll sign this document as well.

While this can seem like an overwhelming amount of paperwork, it becomes less so with each investment. However, it's always prudent to have your attorney review the documents. He or she has likely seen thousands of these partnerships and can help you make changes or guide you as necessary. A good attorney on the front end will always be worth the money.

Protect Your Children's Future

Another good reason to have a lawyer on your team is to set up your estate plan.

As of 2018, $11.2 million is exempt from estate taxes at the time of your death.[50] That number applies to both you and your spouse, so currently you can pass $22.4 million to your children tax-free if your estate is properly structured. Many of you will read that and assume you'll never eclipse that number. That may be true, but let's consider some history.

In 2017, the estate tax exemption was $5.49 million. In 2001, it was $675,000. Those are big swings, and with a government that is currently running out of money, your kids' inheritance is going to look very appealing. There are forces out there that vilify the rich and want to redistribute the wealth of the country. A quick law change could easily wipe out the current estate tax exemption and could leave your children with much less than you planned.

> **► ACTION ITEM ◄**
> Consult an estate attorney to review or create
> your estate plan.

So even if you aren't thinking of yourself, consider your children. There are ways to arrange a full transfer of assets and cash flow at your passing that will have minimal tax effect on your heirs. Not only can you create a life of choices and control for yourself, but you can pass that legacy on to your children and maybe even their children. Other than your love, there can be no greater gift than to secure their future so they can thrive and contribute to the world.

Beyond Asset Protection

On a final note, while asset protection is a key component in your journey to financial freedom, your attorneys will play other roles as well. You might need help in real estate, business, litigation, estate planning, or other areas. Just like doctors, lawyers specialize and possess different expertise.

To put it into context, if you have a broken bone, you'll see an orthopedic surgeon and if you have cancer, you'll seek out the best oncologist you can find. Many times, a generalist won't have the expertise for your specific medical needs. In the same way, a legal generalist may not have the requisite knowledge for your business needs. You must seek out specialists. If you don't know where to find them, ask someone who has done what you want to do. They'll know where to find the right legal help.

Whatever path you decide to follow, resist the urge to "go it alone." Consult your attorney about which strategy is right for you. As a member of your team, your attorney will guide you and protect your assets.

Expert Advice

My goal with this book is to deliver the best education possible to support your journey to financial freedom. With that in mind, I felt that the most efficient way to bring you legal information was to enlist a true expert. The adjunct section written below is produced by corporate attorney Garrett Sutton. Mr. Sutton is an asset protection specialist, author of numerous books on the subject, a sought-after speaker, and most importantly, one of my asset protection attorneys. Based on my personal experience, I am confident that the information below will save you time, money, and heartache.

Garrett Sutton

I'm glad you are reading this chapter. While the legal aspect of your long-term financial plan may not be the most exciting, it's a crucial part of your strategy. You don't want to build up your net worth only to have someone take it all away. This happens far too often in our litigious world. Unfortunately, our school system doesn't teach us how to protect our assets with legal safeguards. Fortunately, all 50 states allow for the creation of entities (or separate "legal beings") that will protect your assets. With that in mind, below is a brief overview of the options available to protect and defend your hard-earned assets and investments.

The Good, the Bad, and the Ugly

Starting with the Bad, the worst way to hold title to assets such as real estate, brokerage accounts, paper assets, and precious metals is in your individual name. This gives you no protection. If you get into a conflict or a lawsuit and a judgment is rendered against you, assets held in your name are easily reached.

Other Bad ways to own assets include joint tenancies, tenants in common (absent an LLC), living trusts, and land trusts. Joint tenancy and "tenants in common" are words that you will sometimes see on bank and investment agreements. The simple explanation is that with these two structures, every partner is responsible for 100 percent of the liability. That means your partner could do something wrong or illegal and you can be held liable for all his actions. Your liability isn't limited and these structures should be avoided.

There is also a great deal of misinformation about the next two choices, living trusts and land trusts. Despite the deliberate falsehoods of promoters, living trusts and land trusts do not provide any sort of asset protection. Be very cautious of online sales sites that not only don't guarantee you a fiduciary duty to get it right but don't even know what a fiduciary duty is. This could put your nest egg at risk.

Please stay away from the Bad ways to hold title.

The Ugly way to hold your investment assets is with a C Corporation (C Corp). Beware of promoters advocating this strategy. It's appropriate for big business but a poor way to own personal assets. While it does have a component of asset protection, the C Corp features double taxation. This means your profits are taxed both at the corporate level and when monies are distributed to shareholders. When you sell an asset like an apartment building for a gain, your taxes will be far higher with this double taxation than if you only had a single level of tax. "Flow-through" taxation is a much better strategy.

The Good entities, those that provide the best protection for real assets such as real estate, are the LLC (limited liability company) and the LP (limited partnership). These entities offer both flow-through taxation and, in some states, strong asset protection. (There are slight differences between a real estate and an "operating" business.)

The difference between LLCs and LPs is the number of entities needed for complete protection. In an LLC, everyone within the structure of the entity is protected, so only one entity is needed. In contrast and by definition, an LP requires two partners: a general partner and a limited partner. The general partner has unlimited liability for the LP's operations. As an individual, you don't want to carry that risk. You want to convert that unlimited liability into a limited liability entity such as a corporation or LLC. This means setting up two entities for an LP to really protect your assets. The LLC and LP structures are represented below.

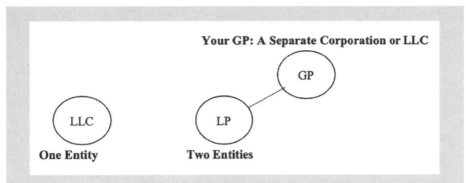

Today, due to their simplicity, many investors use LLCs for their asset protection needs; however, there are uses for the LP. In the Limited Partnership structure, the general partner entity, with as little as 2 percent ownership, can control all the partnership activities without interference from the other limited partners. This provides certainty of control, and if that's important, you would consider an LP.

It's also important to note that all states are not created equal regarding asset protection laws. In some states, such as California, New York, and Utah, the laws don't provide as much protection, while states such as Wyoming have very strong laws that work in favor of the entity owner. Your attorney can set up your entities in the state of your choice.

Asset Protection in Action

Let's assume you have read this book, taken the advice in this section, and contacted an asset protection attorney. Your assets are now protected in a limited liability entity that is formed in a state with strong asset protection laws. How will your assets be protected in the event of an attack on your resources?

If you had a problem at a property, or were at fault in a significant car wreck, and insurance didn't cover the claim, the victim's attorney is going to try to collect from any source possible. He will first look at your personal assets. As mentioned, if a title is held in your own name or that of a land trust, living trust, or personal tenancy in common, that attorney can easily reach the asset. Fortunately, you properly structured your legal entities. Let's look at how the scenario plays out with an LLC. (It's the same for LPs but we will use LLCs from here on).

First, we need to distinguish between the types of attacks. A tenant suing over a condition of a property is an inside attack. If the plaintiff prevails and there is inadequate insurance coverage, they can reach the equity inside the LLC. This is true in all 50 states.

This is also a good illustration of why you should not put multiple properties in one LLC. If you lose a lawsuit over one property, the plaintiff can attack all the properties held in that LLC. If you are going to lose, it's better to lose on one property than ten. Separation of your assets provides that protection.

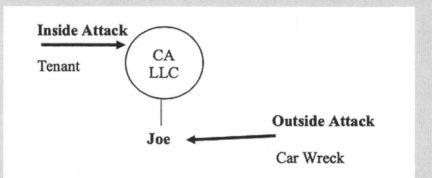

Outside attacks are where the weak vs. strong state issue comes into play. Under California, New York, Utah, and other weak-state laws, the car wreck victim can force a sale of the asset held by the LLC in order to collect. This puts your property at risk and is not effective asset protection.

The way forward is to have the weak-state LLC held by a strong state Wyoming LLC. As such, the structure looks like this:

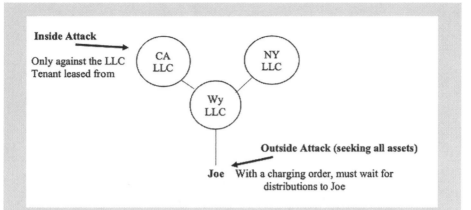

The benefit of setting up your LLC in a strong state is that it recognizes and utilizes what is called a "charging order." A charging order is the exclusive collection remedy available to the car wreck victim in strong states like Wyoming, Nevada, and Delaware. It is a lien on distributions. Unlike a weak state such as California, where the victim can force a sale of the asset, the charging order limits them to receiving whatever the Wyoming LLC distributes to "Joe" (who is part of the LLC). The victim is "charged" with the receipt of Joe's distribution.

But what if Joe doesn't receive anything? What if the California and New York LLC don't distribute any monies to the Wyoming LLC? Then Joe gets nothing and, accordingly, neither does the car wreck victim.

This is the position you want to be in. Attorneys work on a contingency fee basis. In most cases, they only get paid when money is collected. It's not a good use of their time to get a charging order in Wyoming and have to monitor whether distributions have been made. They would rather work on the next case involving easy-to-reach insurance monies. Knowing this, we structure your holdings with a blocking Wyoming LLC.

While initially all this may seem confusing, these are sound and tested business practices. You don't need to have all the answers because your asset protection attorney will guide you through the process. © 2020 CorporateDirect.com.

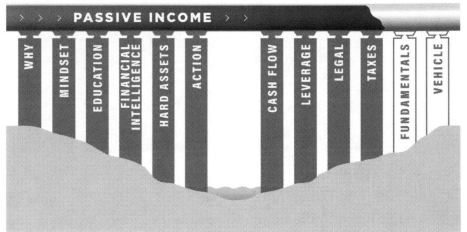

BUILDING YOUR
PASSIVE INCOME PIPELINE

YOUR
NOW

YOUR
FUTURE

PASSIVE INCOME

WHY
MINDSET
EDUCATION
FINANCIAL INTELLIGENCE
HARD ASSETS
ACTION
CASH FLOW
LEVERAGE
LEGAL
TAXES
FUNDAMENTALS
VEHICLE

Chapter 13

Keep More of Your Money

The only difference between death and taxes is that death doesn't get worse every time Congress meets.

—WILL ROGERS

I t's summer 2012. The race for the U.S. presidency is in full swing and the mud is flying. Democrat Barack Obama is squared off against Republican Mitt Romney. An advertisement from the Obama campaign begins with the words, "You work hard, stretch every penny, but chances are you pay a higher tax rate than him: Mitt Romney made $20 million dollars in 2010, but paid only 14 percent in taxes—probably less than you."[51]

Flash forward four years to September 26, 2016. Donald Trump and Hillary Clinton are participating in their first debate in their respective bids to be the next President of the United States. During the contentious exchange, Mr. Trump is accused of not paying taxes on his income. His response: "That's because I'm smart."[52]

The less tax you pay, the more money you keep for yourself, which provides an immediate financial return.

The subject of taxes often creates intense controversy. I hate to pay taxes but don't get me wrong. Our tax dollars fund necessary services and I pay them promptly when they are due. I just don't have to like it.

I'm sure you don't enjoy paying taxes either. Taxes are your biggest expense, and they cause leaks in your pipeline. The more you pay, the less money available for your personal needs. Conversely, the less tax you pay, the more money you keep for yourself, which provides an immediate financial return.

The question is: Do you have a moral or legal obligation to "pay your fair share"?

Legally Avoiding Taxes

While we are bound to follow the rules of the land, it turns out that every citizen has the legal right to pay as low a tax as possible. Consider this quote from Judge Learned Hand, from the U.S. Court of Appeals for the Second Circuit, in *Gregory v. Helvering*: "Any one may so arrange his affairs that his taxes shall be as low as possible; he is not bound to choose that pattern which will best pay the Treasury; there is not even a patriotic duty to increase one's taxes."[53]

The point is that, while it's illegal to evade taxes, it's entirely legal, and even encouraged, to avoid them. There is no legal or moral obligation to pay more taxes than the law requires. Why would I pay more than I have to?

Newsflash: *The U.S. is a tax haven.* It is one of the most tax-friendly developed countries in the world.[54] There are countries with even more attractive tax laws, such as Bermuda, Monaco, and the United Arab Emirates but be prepared to move there if you wish to take advantage of that.[55]

In the meantime, Uncle Sam provides plenty of options to pay less taxes provided you know how to utilize them. This is why it's so important to have a CPA or tax advisor on your team. They understand the intricacies of the material I broadly sketch out below and can help you navigate the complexities of the tax code.

Partner with the Government

The United States Tax Code and its supporting case law weigh in at around 70,000 pages.[56] Buried in those thousands of pages are laws and rules designed not just to generate revenue for the government but to guide the population to do the things the government wants. For example, housing, stable businesses, and energy are mainstays of the economy, so the government incentivizes its citizens to produce them.

While it's illegal to evade taxes, it's entirely legal, and even encouraged, to avoid them.

When it comes to housing, there are tax incentives for those who are willing to take the risk of building homes and apartments. Buildings are required to house companies and to store products. Thus, there are real estate deductions for office buildings and warehouses.

The government's most magical tax gift is depreciation. Depreciation is a "phantom loss" that you can take advantage of each year. If you own a building, the government assumes it will deteriorate and lose value. The IRS typically allows you to write off some of that value when completing your yearly tax returns. For a residential property, the depreciation is calculated over a 27.5-year period; for commercial real estate, it's spread out over 39 years.

In round numbers, if you owned a $1 million commercial building, you would show roughly $25,000 of phantom loss every year. If your income from the property was $50,000 that year, you would only pay taxes on $25,000. In this simple example, that equates to $25,000 of tax-deferred income—deferred for as long as you own the property. (These numbers are not completely accurate and are used for illustrative purposes only.)

That is just the basic deduction for depreciation. As Tom Wheelwright explains a few pages further on, new laws allow for significantly more tax savings due to "cost-segregation" and "bonus depreciation."

I find depreciation so exciting that I used to enthusiastically show my wife how much money I "lost" each year when I got my real estate statements. She thought I was crazy because she knew we had cashed checks from those investments. Once I explained the magic of tax deductions, she understood. It meant there was more for us!

The government's most magical tax gift is depreciation. Depreciation is a "phantom loss" that you can take advantage of each year.

Other beneficial tax breaks are available in real estate that can bring your taxable income down, even to zero in some cases. For example, if arranged properly, you can defer 100 percent of your taxes on a property sale if you utilize what's called a 1031 tax exchange. This section of the tax code allows you to sell your property and defer the tax payment if you re-invest the proceeds into a property with value that is greater than or equal to the property you sold.[57] I'm not an accountant so consult your advisors, but I know from personal experience that it's possible to legally pay little or no tax when you own real estate.

Small and large businesses are the backbone of the economy, so there are tax incentives and deductions for running them. Any legal business can deduct expenses against revenue, which lowers the tax burden. Most of you do this in your practice if you are the owner. If you're an employee, you don't have access to these benefits.

Energy is required to run our economy, so there are deductions and credits designed to encourage energy production, innovation, and exploration. The government provides tax breaks for oil drillers, for example. If you invest in an oil well, you'll be able to deduct up to 80 percent of your investment in the first year due to what are called "intangible drilling costs" (IDC's).[58] This provides an almost immediate return on your investment, especially if you are in a high tax bracket. There are even more incentives to take that deduction to almost 100 percent in the ensuing years.

I'm not suggesting that you invest in speculative oil investments or buy an apartment building solely for the tax benefits. You should never let the tax tail wag the dog. But you should also know that every investment has different tax implications, some of which can positively affect your financial return and your choice of investment vehicles.

These are just a few brief examples of the benefits of understanding the tax system or having an advisor who does. These benefits are available to you—but maybe not in your present situation. Read on.

Doctors and Taxes

Prior to 1986, one of the favorite investments for doctors was tax-advantaged property that could be used to offset physician wages. Back then, you could invest in a bad project that lost money, but the loss could be used to offset normal income from your medical practice. It was a great deal and it didn't matter if the investment itself made money. Unfortunately, the Tax Reform Act of 1986 took that deduction away.[59] No longer could physicians invest in money-losing real estate deals and still write off the losses against their medical income. Where did that leave us?

Previously, I discussed the Cashflow Quadrant™ and how it represents the way we produce our income. As doctors, we make our income on the left side of that quadrant which ties our hands from a tax standpoint. As you can see by the graphic below, the way we make our income also influences the amount of tax we pay.

CASHFLOW Quadrant was created by Robert Kiyosaki. To learn more about the power of CASHFLOW Quadrant, go to www.richdad.com. Used with permission of CASHFLOW Technologies, Inc. All rights reserved. This grant of permission is not an endorsement of Tom Burns, or the content of this book.

In general, those in the Employee and Self-employed Quadrants pay a higher percentage of taxes on their income than those in the Business Owner and Investor Quadrants. As doctors, most of our income is derived from salary, either paid from revenues or paid by our employers. This puts us in the E or S Quadrant—the most highly taxed income category. This is W-2 income and additional taxes such as Social Security and Medicare are layered on top of the federal rate. Taxes are generally lower in the B and I Quadrants and often Social Security and Medicare taxes do not apply.

What are your options?

If you are a W-2 employee, your options are limited. The income derived from a W-2 occupation is called "ordinary income" and is taxed at the highest marginal rate. However, if you are an investor, a whole new world of opportunity becomes available to you. Investor income is frequently derived from portfolio or passive income and is often taxed at lower rates. In addition, passive income can be offset by passive losses. As you add various investments to your portfolio, the positive effect on your tax burden multiplies.

Another option is to obtain "real estate professional" status. If acquired, this can allow you to offset ordinary income from your medical practice with passive losses from your real estate. You must qualify for this designation and there are strict requirements established by the IRS. If you wish to know more about real estate professional status, visit www. richdoctor.com/tools.

I was not aware of any of these options early in my career. When I got my first paycheck, my impression was that taxes were an ever-present reality. As I made my first few investments in the real estate world, I started to notice some changes in my taxes.

I was making money in real estate, but it didn't seem to get taxed as heavily as my physician salary. As my portfolio grew, the income grew. And yet, when my real estate and investment income was added to my physician income, my blended tax rate went down. Currently, my tax rate typically lands in the single digits to mid-teens. I am working on getting it legally down to zero!

> *It is important to realize that to become rich it is not how much*
> *money you make, but how much you keep.*

Imagine keeping 80-100 percent of your income and how that might change your lifestyle. You could buy more, do more, work less! The choice will be yours. That's the benefit of understanding money, taxes, and investments. That's how you become a rich doctor. Knowledge of the tax laws and an expert advisor will help you do that.

It is important to realize that to become rich it is not how much money you make, but how much you keep. So even as a physician, you can take advantage of tax benefits that are available to the very wealthiest of individuals. Keep more of your money and accelerate your journey to financial freedom.

Next Steps

If you are like me, you like to get a good deal on products and services. I love getting stuff on sale, but when it comes to professional advice, I suggest you pay top dollar. The old saying, "You get what you pay for," is absolutely true in the world of tax advice.

Resist the urge to have your brother-in-law do your taxes just to save a few bucks. In the long run, it could cost you many times more than your perceived savings. I still sometimes complain about the prices my advisors charge. Then I realize this is poor doctor thinking. Inevitably, down the line, I discover that their expert advice has made or saved me many times more than the cost of their service. Pay for your advice and pay for the best. I pay a high price for my advice, but the value received has been more than worth it.

> ### ▶ ACTION ITEM ◀
> Hire a CPA and/or a tax advisor and proactively discuss tax-saving strategies.

My job is not to know the tax code inside and out. My job is to identify investments that make economic sense and bring me closer to my personal financial goals. Although it helps to have a broad understanding of tax consequences, it's my advisor's job to guide me and obtain the maximum tax benefit. He's the one who stays up at night reading lines of tax code that would put most people to sleep!

Taxes are your biggest expense. Reducing or eliminating them pays immediate returns. Your tax advisor is one of the most important members of your team, so choose one carefully and do your due diligence. Employing a skilled tax advisor is a prime example of leveraging the knowledge of someone else. Use your own time to do what you do best, whether it's treating patients or finding another cash flow-producing investment!

Expert Advice

As in the previous chapter on legal issues, I feel obligated to provide you with advice straight from an expert. I am not an accountant and don't provide accounting advice. I can put taxes in the context of the medical profession, but Tom Wheelwright, my tax advisor, is a genuine authority. He's the author of the book, *Tax-Free Wealth*, which is a must-read for anyone seeking financial freedom. He is a sought-after speaker and a renowned expert on the subject of taxes. This is high-level information offered for the mere price of a book. It may be the best deal you get this year!

Tom Wheelwright, CPA

Taxes are fundamentally a set of incentives for business owners and investors. Under the current U.S. law, you will only be taxed on the portion of your income that you don't reinvest (which essentially means we have a consumption tax). This only works when you reinvest directly into income-producing assets such as your business, real estate, or commodities. Paper assets do not provide the same tax benefits since paper is merely a derivative of the actual business.

Many of you put a lot of money back into your business. We call these business expenses. Pretty much anything can be a business expense so long as you meet four simple tests.

1. There must be a business purpose. This simply means that there is some real business reason for the expenditure. This is a pretty easy test to meet for most expenses of your business.

2. The expense must be ordinary. Another word for ordinary is "typical." Is this expense typical as to type, amount, and frequency? For example, it may be typical for an insurance salesman to treat his best client to a fancy dinner with an expensive bottle of wine. A CPA doing the same with his best client may not be so typical (since CPA stands for Cheapest People in America).

3. The expense must be necessary. This means that the expense either is likely to create profit or that it will expand the market for the business.

4. The expense must be properly documented. This includes a receipt and, in the case of meals, includes a notation of the parties involved, the date, the location, and the purpose of the meeting (or topic of discussion). A credit card statement does not meet this requirement, so be sure to scan and file the actual receipt. Remember that if you pretend to document your expense, you will get a pretend deduction. The IRS, in recent years, has been a stickler for proper documentation.

One way to look at this is that if the expense is good for your business, it's deductible. If it's not good for your business, it's probably not deductible. If you focus on those expenses that will be good for your business, you will reduce your taxes and, at the same time, improve your business.

What changed under the 2017 Tax Act is that reinvesting the money in producing assets now also creates a deduction. Prior to 2017, if earnings were invested in assets (an asset being anything that produces benefit over a long period of time and that would typically show up on your balance sheet—as opposed to your income statement), you would only receive a small benefit each year to correspond with the income being produced by the asset. For example, if you purchased a building, you would only receive a deduction of 5 to 10 percent per year for depreciation. Now when you purchase an asset, you receive an immediate tax benefit. Here are a couple of important examples.

1. Real estate—When you purchase investment or business real estate, you essentially buy four categories of assets. You buy the land, the building, the land improvements (paving and landscaping), and the contents of the building (flooring, window coverings, cabinetry, appliances). The land does not wear out, so there is no deduction for the land. The building wears out over a long period of time, so the deduction is limited to less than 4 percent each year. The land improvements wear out slightly faster, so the depreciation rate is 5-10 percent. The contents wear out even faster and receive a depreciation rate of 20 percent. Under "bonus depreciation," you can depreciate 100 percent of the land improvements and contents in the first year. This is a substantial acceleration of the deduction for an asset that should produce income for many years.

2. Inventory—Historically, a business could only deduct the cost of inventory at the time it was sold. The new law allows a small business (under $25 million of sales) to deduct much of the inventory when it's purchased. This is an incentive for small businesses to grow and add inventory.

There are thousands of tax benefits to be found in the law. The great majority of the tax law is dedicated to reducing taxes through these incentives. Since we are already partners with the government (check out the withholding on your next paycheck), why not be good partners and do what the government wants us to do and reduce our taxes as a result? Remember that the fastest way to put money in your pocket is to reduce your biggest expense—taxes! ©2019 On The Lake Holdings, LLC.

BUILDING YOUR
PASSIVE INCOME PIPELINE

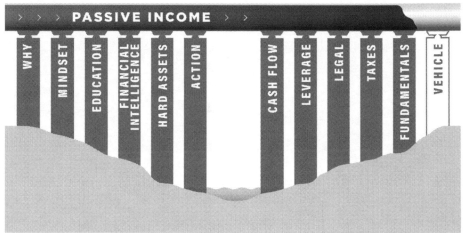

Chapter 14

Fundamentals and Guidelines

You can have all the physical ability in the world, but you still have to know the fundamentals.

—MICHAEL JORDAN

M oney has a unique language with terms and concepts that aren't a part of everyday communication. This is similar to the language we use in medicine. We spend years learning to speak in medical terms, but our patients don't have the same training. If your patient doesn't understand the words you are using, he or she won't be able to follow your guidance for their health.

Likewise, if you want to learn about money and passive income, you'll need to understand the vocabulary and the context. In this chapter, I will expose you to some of the terms, structures, and situations you will encounter so you can converse intelligently with your advisors and members of your investment team.

The terms and facts presented below are based on the hundreds of questions about hard assets and cash flow investing that I have fielded over the years from colleagues and investors. The list is more practical than comprehensive, but it gives you information you can use immediately and enough foundational knowledge for new situations that may arise in the future.

Passive vs. Active Investing

Throughout the book, I've discussed passive income and its supreme utility in creating rich doctors. Passive income is the essential component in your financial freedom machine. It can be produced through active participation or as a passive investor. (That sounds confusing, but active effort can produce long-term passive income.) The method you choose depends on how fast you want to go and which path fits your goals.

When speaking to doctors about creating income using vehicles outside of the stock market, one of the first things I often hear is, "I'm busy enough as a doctor. I don't have time to fix toilets or run another business." That's an understandable reaction, but if you don't understand the options available, you will be limiting your own success. Without knowing what is possible, you might quit before you get started.

My first response is that if you want to change the circumstances of your life, you must do it yourself. No one will do it for you. According to motivational speaker Denis Waitley, "There are two primary choices in life: To accept conditions as they exist or accept the responsibility for changing them." The choice is yours; you are in charge.

Having said that, I can reassure you that you don't need to fix toilets if you don't want to. There are mechanisms available that can increase your passive income and don't require inordinate amounts of time. You can still do your job as a professional while creating your passive income stream.

In broad terms, you can be a passive or an active investor. Each has its pros and cons. The following is a broad summary of each.

Active Investing: If you want to become more involved and have more control over your assets, you can be an active investor. This doesn't mean you have to repair plumbing, take calls from tenants, or run the business by yourself. It means that you find the opportunities, put the deal together, and manage the investment. You then hire the people to repair the plumbing. That's the path I chose because it fit my personality.

As I discussed earlier, I chose real estate as my vehicle. The deals were small at first and could be accomplished while practicing full-time as an orthopedic surgeon. Over time, I developed an expertise in those markets and was able to multiply my original successes. I hired managers to deal with day to day management, so I only had to do the work once. Some of those properties have paid me for 20 years. Eventually the projects got larger, I found partners, and we started taking investors. It grew from there to the point where we now manage a portfolio worth hundreds of millions of dollars.

Active investing provides more control than passive investing but requires more time and education.

If you are like me and have the drive to go bigger and better, then active investing may be the right strategy. You don't need to start big. In fact, you should start small so your mistakes will be less costly. My first property was a single condominium at a major university. I didn't know what I was doing, but I learned fast. You can do the same thing and it doesn't have to be in real estate. You may have talents in other areas that you want to exploit. Explore those opportunities and act on them if you feel it's right for you.

Active investing provides more control than passive investing but requires more time and education. It depends on where your heart lies. The effort was worth it for me and I'm confident that it will be for you if that is the path you choose.

Passive Investing: Passive investing is simply placing money with another person or group that is actively managing an investment. If you are the passive investor, you have minimal decision-making control, but you also do none of the work. It's the path many professionals take when they decide to supplement their income.

For doctors who are often stressed and overworked with limited free time, it can make a lot of sense. And because, as physicians, you typically have more income than expenses, passive investing provides a golden opportunity that many people don't have.

I know plenty of doctors who have created large streams of income exclusively through passive investments. They've discovered someone who actively creates and manages hard asset investments and leveraged that symbiotic relationship to create cash flow. One surgeon I know invested almost exclusively with a group specializing in apartment complexes. Over a period of ten years, he produced enough passive cash flow to match his surgical income. All this was done while he practiced medicine full-time.

Although my time involves actively managing real estate projects for our investors, I also passively invest with others. Sometimes it's nice to let someone else do the work! One way or another, I want to see more and more dollars flowing into my accounts each month without requiring my effort. Usually I invest with people who have experience in markets and industries that are outside my area of expertise.

So, if you have funds to invest, you can participate in true cash flow investing without impacting your work or personal life. Frankly, many physicians I know use a purely passive strategy to create extra income streams. After all, we're busy caring for people and spending time with our families. But never fear; there's an investing team out there for you.

Passive Investing with a Sponsor

If you're going to become a passive investor, you'll often start by participating with a sponsor through a syndication, as first presented in an earlier chapter. I'll discuss the process in more detail here so you'll be better prepared when the opportunity arises.

A sponsor, or syndicator, is a person or group that finds the deal and packages all the pieces together in a neat bundle for investors. The sponsor is typically the General Partner or the Managing Partner of the entity that owns the project and is responsible for everything associated with it.

Although this was touched on earlier, it bears repeating: A syndication is a model in which one person, or a group of people, puts together an opportunity and offers proportional ownership to multiple investors. In that model, the sponsor uses investor capital to acquire an asset that he otherwise could not have bought on his own. The investor relies on the sponsor's time, experience, and expertise to put his or her capital to work. It's the positive use of leverage for both parties.

Passive investing through the syndication model is an efficient way to leverage your time and create cash flow.

Before the investment is ever made available to you, the sponsor spends money and time looking at multiple projects before eventually uncovering a viable opportunity. Drawing on their specific expertise, he or she then creates a business plan that will produce a good return for the investors. This is often called "due diligence."

As compensation for this due diligence, the sponsor typically receives a disproportionate share of the profits relative to his initial contribution. The profit split depends on the type of investment and the philosophy of the sponsor, but to give an example, investors might supply 100 percent of the money while profits are split 80 percent to the investors and 20 percent to the sponsor. This bothers some investors but it's a fair trade.

The sponsor trades his time and risks his money to find a project that has the potential to make a profit for everybody. In return, the passive investors collectively give up a small fraction of the return to compensate that effort. This is one of the multiple ways to split up cash flow between sponsors and passive investors. It's a predetermined straight split between sponsor and investor that begins with dollar one of profit.

Another form of profit split is the "preferential return." In this model, there will still be a predetermined split of profits between sponsor and investor. However, the split doesn't start until the investor receives a contracted percentage of return. This would be similar to the interest that you are paid on a savings account. This assures the investor that, at a minimum, he or she will receive the first dollars that come out of an investment no matter how well it performs. This aligns the interests of the sponsor and investor on a deeper level because the sponsor receives no distribution until the property performs well enough to eclipse the required preferential return.

The sponsor will often receive income for managing the investment in the form of fees. This provides the sponsor the means to find more opportunities for you to invest in. They should be explained and disclosed before you make your investment. Fees vary on a case-by-case basis and can include acquisition, management, equity, and debt fees in various combinations based on the total value of the property or the project.

Don't be put off by *reasonable* fees paid at the beginning of a transaction but do be cognizant of high fees. If you feel the fees are high, ask the sponsor to explain each one and compare them to industry norms. The sponsor shouldn't make a killing on the front end of a deal and should also be sharing your risk. Most of his profit should be realized only after the investors make their money back.

Passive investing through the syndication model is an efficient way to leverage your time and create cash flow. The investor with little time or experience uses the time, knowledge, experience, and effort of the sponsor. In return, the sponsor, who doesn't have all the capital needed for the investment, leverages the money of the investor. In the end, if it's a successful project, both parties come out on top.

What Makes a Good Sponsor?

There are good and bad sponsors and they will both come to you with opportunities to invest. My goal is to help you know the difference between the two. There are also countless ways to structure a deal between a sponsor and the investors, and while there is no one "best way," there are a few things to look for.

In most hard asset syndications, the sponsor will invest alongside the investors. That money will be treated exactly the same as the investor money is treated (other than the sponsor's disproportionate share of profits from his General Partner ownership). This should be a comfort to you as the investor. If the sponsor is willing to risk his or her own money on a project, it's a good sign that he or she's confident it will work. It's not a guarantee of success, but at least you can feel more comfortable about entrusting your hard-earned money with this person.

It's not a hard and fast rule but be cautious about investing in a project in which the sponsor doesn't. You want their interests aligned with yours: If the deal goes well, they make money. If it goes bad, they don't. And beware of structures that allow the sponsor to profit even if you make no money. In my experience, the fairest structure pays the investors first or at least the lion's share of the profits. Good sponsors take care of their investors first.

Although past performance does not guarantee future success, the sponsor's track record indicates their level of experience and how they have treated their investors. If they've been through both good times and bad, their experience often allows them to see trouble before it appears. If they've treated their previous investors fairly—a sponsor should be willing to give you plenty of references—there will be no shortage of past clients to provide testimonials. It can ease your mind to speak with someone who has done business with a sponsor and continues to invest with them.

There are good and bad sponsors and they will both come to you with opportunities to invest.

Sometimes a sponsor is just starting out and has no previous projects, which means there are no past results to review and no previous investors to talk to. That's not always a bad thing. Good sponsors need to start somewhere. However, if it's their first deal, that sometimes translates to better proportional ownership for the investor group.

A good sponsor should never have an issue with giving you information about a proposed investment or one you currently participate in. Transparency is important. After all, you own part of the project so you are entitled to review the financial information. You may not want to pour through rent rolls and financial statements, but they should be available if requested. Be wary of sponsors who hesitate to give you information about a deal you are a part of.

Typically, a seasoned sponsor will provide monthly or quarterly updates on your project. This usually comes in the form of regular e-mails to all the investors. It will include a narrative of how the project is going with data (as available) to back it up. A good sponsor communicates frequently.

You also want your sponsor to be focused. Expertise in a certain area can lead to better deals and might help to avoid losses. If the sponsors have deep knowledge about a market or industry, they sometimes get "insider" opportunities that can increase your return because they pick up a deal for a discount. If they've been in the industry long enough, they will have experienced up markets and down markets. They can use that experience to help avoid bad deals.

Unfortunately, not every investment deal goes as planned. Most sponsors have had failures somewhere along the line and, frankly, are probably better investors because of those missteps. If they've had projects that didn't go as planned, they should be willing to tell you about them and what they learned in the process. If they've been in the business for a reasonable amount of time and haven't had a bad project, dig deeper to make sure they are giving you the whole story.

Even if you find that they've never had a bad deal, ask them about the things that could cause the current opportunity to be unsuccessful. You want to know that they've thought about potential problems. Their answers will reveal their understanding of the market they're in.

As an example, I was once approached by a new syndicator who was buying apartments and upgrading them to increase rental rates and, thus, the value of the property. It was a good strategy and had been successful over the previous decade. Because it was widely believed that we were at the top of that market, though, I asked about potential problems such as increased vacancy, declining rents, and rising interest rates. His answer was that apartments always go up in value and his plan was to sell for a profit. He reiterated that a recession would not affect the apartment market.

I was intrigued by his confidence, so I dug a little deeper. His primary occupation was sales and he had just started investing in multi-family properties two years earlier after taking a seminar on how to purchase apartments. He had never been through a recession as a real estate investor and had never invested in anything prior to that. Based on current data, he was buying into the top of the market.

While his plan was sound in the current strong environment, he had no back-up strategy for a potential decline in the industry. His plan was based on ever-increasing real estate values and an assumed sale. When asked what he would do if there was a recession, he simply said it would not affect his property.

While I admired his confidence, I prefer to place my bets with someone who has real-world experience. There were plenty of people who felt insulated before the Great Recession in 2008 yet still lost their properties. Someone who's experienced in the world of investing knows that circumstances can change and affect your exit strategy.

A good sponsor will either have multiple exit strategies or will be prepared to hold the asset for an extended period of time. Thus, they will have less chance of getting burned by a downturn in the market. They avoid the trap of thinking, "It will be different this time."

Another quality of good sponsors is availability. If you have a question or an issue, there should always be someone you can contact to discuss your concerns. As mentioned before, not every project goes as planned. It's comforting to know you have quick access to the sponsor for an explanation of any circumstance.

Nobody is perfect and these rules are not set in stone, but they can serve as guidelines for your journey. Practically speaking, you'll often find that you invest with people who have been referred by friends. Even though you may trust your friends, I suggest you still use these guidelines to get more comfortable with the sponsor. Resist the urge to let someone dazzle you with shiny marketing material. Check them out!

What Makes a Good Investment?

At the very highest level, a good investment makes you money and a bad one loses money. That's common sense. Beyond that, asking what makes a good investment is almost like asking if it's better to be a doctor or a lawyer or if the better ice cream is chocolate or vanilla. It depends on the individual investment and the individual investor.

Since you have gotten this far in the book, you know the importance of defining your investment goals. It could be a large bucket of money, passive cash flow, or asset appreciation. Although I favor cash flow, none is empirically better than the other. Different investment types will satisfy different goals.

Still, there are some things to consider. Since this is primarily a passive cash flow book, we will start there. If you are investing for cash flow, you want to have a positive "cash-on-cash" return on your investment. This is typically expressed as a ratio of your cash return divided by your initial investment and is calculated annually. For example, if you invested $10,000 in a project and received $1,100 in dividends or distributions in the first year, your cash-on-cash return would be 11 percent.

Your returns will depend on asset type, market conditions, and deal execution. When times are good, you'll be able to search for higher returns. When times are bad, you will need to adjust your expectations.

> ▶ **ACTION ITEM** ◀
> Learn the key investment metrics and determine how you
> will compare investment opportunities to fit your goals.

Another common term is Return on Investment (ROI). ROI takes into account cash flow, deductions, loan amortization, and price appreciation. In the previous example, if you invested $100,000 and your share was worth $12,000 at the end of the year, your ROI would be 12 percent. You won't end up with the full 12 percent in your pocket, though, because that 12 percent represents both cash flow *and* the increase in the value of the asset. Still, it lets you know your investment is growing. If things go well, one day you'll be able to harvest those remaining profits if there is a sale or refinance of the property.

Some people say that the quicker you get your money back, the better. This is measured by a term called the Internal Rate of Return (IRR), which considers the time value of money. The higher the IRR, the quicker your return. This creates the assumption that the higher the IRR, the better the investment. This is often but not always true; a high IRR is great, but it doesn't represent the total amount of return.

Consider the two investments in the graphic below: In Project A you invest $100,000 and receive $10,000 in each of the next four years, followed by $100,000 in the final year. Your total return over five years is $140,000, which includes the return of your initial investment, and the IRR is 8 percent. Project B is set up differently: You receive $100,000 in the first year followed by $10,000 in each of the next two years. Your total return over three years is $120,000 which carries an IRR of 16 percent.

$100,000 Invested	Project A Return	Project B Return
Yr 1	$ 10,000	$ 100,000
Yr 2	$ 10,000	$ 10,000
Yr 3	$ 10,000	$ 10,000
Yr 4	$ 10,000	
Yr 5	$ 100,000	
Total Return	$ 140,000	$ 120,000
IRR	8%	16%

Project A has a lower IRR but returns more money; Project B gets you your money back faster but returns less money. So you have to know your investment goals to decide which deal would be best for you. IRR is an important metric but not the only way to evaluate a deal.

The best scenario is to receive your initial investment back as soon as possible and still hold ownership of the asset. For example, you buy 1000 shares of stock at one dollar and it rises to two dollars. If you sell 500 shares for $1,000, you will have recovered your initial investment and you own the remaining 500 shares for free. In this situation, you retain 50 percent of your original ownership but no longer have your initial capital at risk.

In real estate, it's possible to recoup 100 percent of your original investment through a refinance and still own 100 percent of the asset. Some call this an "infinite return". This is an efficient mechanism to get your money back quickly, while increasing the size of your holdings. (For more on the concept of "infinite return," visit www.richdoctor. com/tools.)

Once you get your initial capital back, you can deploy those funds into another project while that initial investment is still working. As your program grows, you will soon have multiple investments working simultaneously. This is how you geometrically grow your cash flow and create financial independence.

In the real estate world, it's possible to recoup 100 percent of your original investment through a refinance and still own 100 percent of the asset.

For the record, I prefer investments that produce stable, regular cash flow. That's how I built my portfolio. As long as there is ongoing cash flow, I don't need to be concerned about the value of an asset or its appreciation from the original purchase price.

Downside protection is another important factor in your choice of investment vehicles. A deal that has a high IRR and cash flow of 20 percent might look great, but it does you no good if it fails before any money is produced. It is thus important to consider the historical gyrations of that particular market and the possibility of unexpected problems. Will that investment be strong enough to weather challenges? The answers are different for each industry and your education will be your defense.

A good investment is one that achieves the goals that you set for your financial plan. If those goals are reached in the timeframe that you've mapped, then you are on your way to financial freedom.

Tax Time as an Investor

I wrote this section separately from the tax chapter because, when we work with new investors, inevitably tax-related questions are generated. If you have never invested in a syndication or a limited liability entity, there will be some tax mechanics that you haven't experienced before.

When you invest with someone else (a sponsor), they assume the responsibility of filing taxes for the investment. In the U.S., what you get at the end of the year is a document called a K-1. This identifies your share of profit and loss relative to your percentage of ownership. The primary thing to know is that you simply need to give this document to your CPA and it will be incorporated into your taxes. If you wish to learn more about what is represented on your K-1, ask your CPA and he or she will likely be happy to explain it to you.

One important point about a K-1 form: While most people know that personal tax returns are due on April 15th, your K-1 may arrive after that date. This tends to freak out first-time investors but it's not uncommon in the investment world. As I mentioned, although I run investments as the General Partner, I also invest passively in other projects and often don't get my last K-1 until late summer. My solution is to file an extension on my taxes every year. It's simple, it doesn't create red flags with the IRS, and your CPA will handle it for you.

Needless to say, if you are investing in your own passive income portfolio, keep good records. Your CPA will be happy, your taxes will be accurate, and you will have a back-up if anybody ever questions you. It's like medical records. If it's not written down or recorded, it never happened. In the tax world, if there is no receipt, there is no deduction.

Taxes are like medical records. If it's not written down, it never happened. In the tax world, if there's no receipt, there's no deduction.

Third-party Review

I find that fresh, experienced eyes are a great way to give me confidence that I am making a good decision. If you find an investment you like, it can be helpful to run it by someone else. That can be a trusted friend, business associate, or CPA. Doing so may keep you from missing something or making an emotional decision.

On the practical side, I typically discuss my investments with my CPA so that I can set them up in the most tax-advantaged way from the beginning. It's not always possible, but this can create significant tax savings when an investment matures.

This is by no means a complete dissertation on the fundamentals of investing. It's more of a primer for those who haven't ventured into private investments and a light review for the more experienced. I've tried to incorporate some common terminology and structures to familiarize you with the process. I have also introduced the operational side so you will generally know what to expect as a passive or an active investor.

As you navigate the world of investing and wealth creation, you'll run across unfamiliar terms and situations. I encourage you to ask questions and research things you don't understand. You'll become more experienced, your decisions will come quicker, and you'll make them with more confidence. After all, you became an experienced doctor. Now you will become an experienced rich doctor!

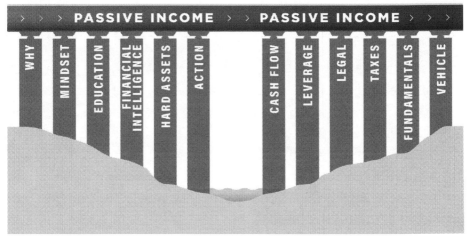

Chapter 15

Choose Your Vehicle

*I'm a great believer in luck, and I find the harder I work
the more I have of it.*

—THOMAS JEFFERSON

Well, you've made it this far in the book and you're ready to put your education to work. Your pipeline is built and you need a vehicle to carry you to your future. There are many ways that the wealthy produce and preserve their wealth. This chapter will expose you to some of those options so that you'll know what is out there to create and preserve *your wealth*.

Real Estate

If you've read this far, it should be no secret that I believe real estate is the most accessible way to create and preserve wealth. In my opinion, it is the number one way to create "rich doctors". My story is only one example of someone who was financially uneducated, yet created lasting financial independence through real estate. For this reason, I am using the author's privilege to put it first!

First, be aware that your financial planner may advise you not to become involved in real estate. You might be told it's a risky "alternative asset." Remember, it's only risky if you are uneducated, and your financial planner may not have real estate experience. In addition, he makes no money when you invest in assets that he doesn't sell.

How alternative is it? Rooms were rented to travelers and land was leased to tenants long before the first stock exchange was formed in 1602 by the Dutch East India Company. Even the Bible documents real estate transactions. The Book of Genesis recounts that Abraham bought a plot of burial land for himself and his family, and it was memorialized with a contract. (*The NIV Study Bible*, Gen. 23:16-20) This may be one of the first deeds recorded and its thousands of years old! So investing in real estate is hardly "alternative." Opportunities will be available as long as someone owns property and someone else wants to use it.

Property ownership is also an excellent tool for creating long-lasting passive income and every bit of passive cash flow that isn't correlated with practicing medicine gets you closer to having the freedom of choice.

Real estate has been good to me personally. However, it hasn't been all rainbows and fairy dust. There have been disappointments and victories. Thankfully, the wins have outweighed the losses and they've given me a chance to chase some dreams. Whether you dabble in real estate or make it your passion, I'm confident it will support your path to financial freedom. Let's start with a broad discussion of the benefits of property ownership.

The Four Pillars of Real Estate

The four primary advantages of real estate are *cash flow, appreciation, depreciation,* and *amortization.* When combined with the judicious use of leverage, these advantages can increase the velocity of your money and create a cash flow stream that will set you free. Investing in real estate doesn't necessarily require large sums of money or a significant allocation of your time. You can purchase your own property or, as discussed in the previous chapter, take advantage of the abilities of an experienced real estate sponsor and let them do the work.

A well-designed real estate project will provide regular cash flow that has nothing to do with seeing patients, completing electronic medical records, performing surgery, or getting up at 2 a.m. to handle an emergency at the hospital. This is true passive income, which is the most important part of your financial freedom plan.

In the early stages of your journey, you might use this extra income to obtain more real estate or invest in other sources of passive cash flow. You are free to choose the options as long as your goal is still to replace your expenses. When you generate enough cash flow, you will quickly have the freedom to eliminate some of the more challenging parts of your medical life.

As discussed in the tax chapter, when you purchase a property, you get tax benefits from deductions and *depreciation*—a "phantom loss" that you are permitted to deduct from your passive income. This allows you to keep more of the cash flow that you make from your properties. Also, if you are using leverage (discussed below), you will typically only use 10-20 percent of your own money and 80-90 percent of the bank's money. The bank isn't interested in those tax benefits; they just want their money back according to your contract. But you'll want to pay as little tax as legally possible (while also making a profit, of course). Thankfully, the bank will allow you to claim 100 percent of the depreciation, helping to maximize your cash flow to further fuel your passive income machine.

A well-designed real estate project will provide regular cash flow that has nothing to do with seeing patients, completing electronic medical records, performing surgery, or getting up at 2 a.m. to handle an emergency at the hospital.

In addition, real estate prices generally (but not always) go up over time. This is called *appreciation*. It's often due to inflation but you can also actively increase the value by upgrading the property. As the property appreciates, your equity increases. If it rises enough, the bank will lend you money again on that same piece of real estate. This is called a refinance and can return part or all of the funds that you originally put into the project, making that money available to invest in another venture. Now you have two properties instead of one, but did not need to come up with more money to buy the second.

There's more. Let's assume you made a $20,000 down payment on a $100,000 rental house and the bank gave you the remaining $80,000. The rent you receive is enough to pay for the mortgage and all the expenses of running the property. Anything extra goes into your bank account. Every month, you make a payment to the bank (with the money your tenant gives you). That payment is broken up into principal and interest. The principal is the amount you borrowed, and interest is the cost of that money. Interest is the bank's profit. Every month, the bank applies your principal payment to the original loan and decreases the amount you owe. You are paying off the loan a little bit at a time using the tenants' rent payment. This decrease in the amount owed is called *amortization*.

The beauty of amortization is that the amount you owe declines each month and somebody else is paying for it! As that loan amount decreases, the percentage of the value of your property that becomes yours free and clear—your *equity* in that property—increases. And if this works for one house, it works even better for five houses, or fifty. This is the magic of leverage, or "good debt."

Each of the four main advantages of real estate is enhanced with the use of leverage. For example, if you wish to pay cash for a $100,000 rental house, you would need to save $100,000. You then must accumulate another $100,000 to buy a second house. Saving that kind of money is difficult or impossible for most people. As a medical professional, you might be able to do it, but it could be years before that next purchase is made and that will slow your progress.

On the other hand, if you obtain an 80 percent loan and pay 20 percent cash, you've only used 20 percent of your available investment money. You get the house and still have $80,000 left. That's enough for a really nice car, right? Well yes, but it's also enough to buy four more houses. Then you would have a portfolio of five houses that you purchased using OPM (other people's money) to pay for 80 percent of it.

I was once told that the secret to wealth in real estate was the number of doors you own. In the above example, the use of leverage allows you to own five times more than you would with cash alone. Now you have five houses giving you 100 percent of the cash flow, depreciation, appreciation, and amortization but you only paid 20 percent of the purchase price for each. That's the beauty of leverage. That's how you increase the velocity of your money and accelerate your journey to financial independence!

Many of you reading this might be thinking that it's just too much to do while working a busy medical schedule. Not to worry. You can bite off small bits at a time and learn as you grow or use the syndication model. Either way, you still get all the benefits.

Others might be thinking that they can do this in an even bigger way. The good news is that you're right! In the world of real estate, patience, persistence, and a little education can build a cash flow pipeline of any size to help you design the life you desire.

Business Ownership

Recently, I was in a camp at 13,800 feet in the Pamir mountains in Tajikistan. It had taken me 65 hours to arrive there from my home in Austin. During that time, I got six hours of fitful sleep on the plane to Istanbul and barely eight hours in a hotel along the Old Silk Road. Our drive from Dushanbe, Tajikistan's capital, was 21 hours on a scary, single-lane, dirt road with no guard rails high above the Panj River. We dodged avalanches, mudslides, and boulders while we stared at the Afghanistan border for 400 km. It was exhausting, but we made it.

My campmates were from all over the United States and we'd been looking forward to this trip for 2 ½ years. As I got to know them and learned a little about their families and their lives, something struck me: Each one owned a business.

One guy was only 41 and had just sold the family glass business. Another owned a company that sold products including gloves, hygiene products, and hand soap to hospitals. The guy from Georgia owned multiple companies but his flagship was a janitorial enterprise. Our oldest traveler owned a shop that built sunrooms. Our youngest companion, who arranged the trip, owned a service business. This was a very expensive trip and each of these guys had paid the money and left their businesses for two weeks to go on a once-in-a-lifetime adventure.

I've already defined one component of wealth as the ability to live well without working. Another hallmark of wealth is the ability to travel and have your business thrive and sometimes grow while you're gone. I used to think that required a title such as a doctor or a lawyer, but I soon discovered that no money was made while the doctor was on vacation. I then assumed you needed to own a high-profile business but none of these guys owned one. Yet they were all veteran travelers with companies that supplied enough cash flow to afford exotic trips.

Another hallmark of wealth is the ability to travel and have your business thrive and sometimes grow while you're gone.

Business ownership is a proven path to wealth that many of the planet's richest people have travelled. According to *Forbes*, most billionaires got that way by owning businesses that focused on finance, retail, manufacturing, technology, food, healthcare, energy, or entertainment.[60]

It takes education, experience, and a commitment of time to create a successful business, but it can be done. I know a Texas doctor who owns fast-food franchises. Another physician built a communication platform for doctors. One medical entrepreneur started his own spine implant company. A young surgeon built a mobile app and eventually sold the company. An abundance of physical and virtual businesses is available to those with the passion and skill set.

As a busy surgeon, I didn't have the time or the knowledge base to own an operating business. I also didn't know enough to know who to trust to run one. This became painfully evident when my business partner and I purchased a restaurant just before the Great Recession of 2008. If the recession wasn't bad enough, our manager decided that drinking at the bar down the street was more fun than managing the restaurant. As the primary owners, we were forced to help run the day-to-day operations until we found a replacement. If it hadn't been for the previous owners coming back to help, the restaurant would have died right there. We simply didn't have the experience.

Restaurant ownership didn't fit my skill set, but it might fit yours. I know several people who do very well in the restaurant space. If you have a talent for business and a good team to support you, it could be your ticket to success.

It's a lot easier to avoid a bad deal than to get out of one
after the ink is dry.

But beware: Unscrupulous people love to prey on doctors for their investment dollars. Before investing in a business, make sure you know who you are working with and have a trusted third party look over the proposal. Don't let the dazzle of partial ownership or the promise of huge profits get in the way of objective evaluation. It's a lot easier to avoid a bad deal than to get out of one after the ink is dry.

Paper Assets

The rich almost always include paper assets among their tools for creating and preserving wealth. Sometimes there is so much money to store that you need the capital markets to house it. The paper market is vast, global, and represents considerably more options than a small portfolio of mutual funds which is what most of us are familiar with. Money held in paper assets is liquid and can be borrowed against to some extent. The leverage of paper is not as great as real estate, but the liquidity is superior.

The paper market includes stocks, bonds, mutual funds, currency trading, options, and hedge funds, to name a few. The wealthy usually have a significant percentage of their wealth in cash, cash equivalents, and fixed-income instruments such as bonds—as high as 45 percent.[61] Add hedge funds and the number reaches 50 percent. Another 20 percent might be stored in commodities with the rest in real estate as noted above.

You can use paper assets to invest in real estate through real estate investment trusts (REITs). These are essentially mutual funds backed by real property. They are traded on the stock exchange and are subject to the same rules as the stock market. I feel compelled to add that this is not direct property ownership and does not follow the theme of this book, which is leveraged passive cash flow.

Gold

When I started writing this book, the price of gold was approximately $1,300/ounce. Harry Dent, the author of multiple books including *The Great Crash Ahead*, has predicted it will drop to $700/ounce.[62] Jim Rickards, Wall Street veteran and the author of *The New Case for Gold*, has said it will rise to as high as $10,000/ounce.[63] If you aren't in the gold business, how do you decide if you should buy it?

This is a tricky subject and it took some time to get it straight in my head. Originally, I didn't like gold because it's not a cash-flowing asset and didn't qualify for my asset box. But I was looking at it the wrong way. My problem was that I considered gold an investment.

Gold is not an investment. Gold is money. This sounds simple but it's a difficult concept to grasp.

It is one of the few assets with no counterparty risk. This means that there is no risk of default from another party. It has inherent value which makes it attractive to many. It's also true portable wealth that you can easily carry in your hands.

Some say gold is insurance against inflation because gold maintains buying power while fiat currencies do not. Remember the discussion of inflation in an earlier chapter? If a currency becomes inflated, it takes more of that currency to buy the same amount of gold. If there is deflation, it requires less. If you follow history, fiat currencies typically weaken in value and the gold price rises relative to that currency. This allows gold to maintain its buying power while the currency buys less.

This is how gold hedges against inflation. It is one way to "de-dollarize" some of your portfolio by taking your money out of a depreciating asset and putting it in an asset that holds purchasing power.

In 2016, *Inc. Magazine* stated that the wealthy preserve their money with gold, rare coins, and usable precious metals, among other assets.[64] Gold preserves the value of your money because it is money. In good times or bad, gold will generally buy the same value of a product no matter what the currency price reflects. In other words, an ounce of gold today will buy a nice suit; 100 years ago, an ounce of gold also bought a nice suit. The Federal Reserve or the Bank of England can print as much money as they want, yet the buying power of gold will remain stable.

In good times or bad, gold will generally buy the same value of a product no matter what the currency price reflects.

As we speak, China and Russia are buying gold by the ton—literally. The wealthy are also buying gold. While I make no recommendations, this might be a trend to explore.

Oil and Gas

Reportedly, 4 percent of the world's billionaires created their wealth in energy and roughly 20 percent of "high net worth" individuals put their money in commodities of which oil and gas are a part.[60, 61]

Individual investors can also participate in oil and gas investments and benefit from the generous deductions that the government offers. That said, these are often speculative investments and you should be prepared for anything. I've participated in several of these investments, winning some but more often losing. Fortunately, those tax benefits helped to ease the pain on the failed ventures and made the winners even better.

Agriculture

Although agriculture might seem more appropriate in the real estate section, I discuss it separately because of the importance of the businesses that utilize the land. The world will always need food and shelter. You can buy your own agricultural property, or you can participate in syndications that offer partial ownership of land producing crops such as timber, coffee, chocolate, fruit and marijuana. These crops are harvested annually and provide a source of passive income.

I once owned a ranch in Africa with three partners. Our crop was indigenous animals. It is a well-known fact that if the animal population in Africa isn't separated and protected from the human population, it will be decimated through unregulated hunting and illegal poaching. Ranches like ours served to repopulate the local fauna. The sale of animals paid for the operating costs while the value of the land increased annually.

Your level of understanding of this investment category, your investment philosophy, and your plan for financial freedom will determine if agriculture will be a part of your portfolio.

Insurance

Insurance is an important part of any investment plan. If you own a house or rental property, you insure it against fire, theft, and floods. You can buy liability insurance to protect your business and your property against losses from accidents and lawsuits. If you're a stock trader, you can buy insurance in the form of options to limit your losses. Ownership of gold can be considered insurance against currency collapse or a decline in the stock market.

While insurance is typically used to protect and preserve wealth, there are other strategies to use it to grow wealth. You can purchase a life insurance policy and then legally overfund it with cash value to provide a tax-advantaged savings vehicle. This gives you a bucket of money that is safe from most creditors. As the balance grows, you can become your own banker, using the cash value to borrow against and flexibly pay it back on your terms, if at all. This could accelerate your wealth-building strategy if you needed extra capital. This is not a mainstay of the typical middle-class wealth plan and the returns aren't high, but if you have extra cash, it can be a way to safely harbor funds.

Another use of insurance is life settlements. A life settlement is the discounted purchase of another person's whole life insurance. Upon the death of the policy holder, the purchaser receives the proceeds from the policy. This may sound disrespectful but it's a service to the policyholder because he or she might need the money now.

Imagine that you had an insurance policy and discovered you had terminal cancer. Financially, your heirs are already taken care of and the insurance money isn't needed after you die. You can sell the policy and use that money right away while you're still alive; the buyer takes over the premiums. Maybe you take that trip you've never had time for or donate to your favorite charity. It's totally voluntary and provides an excellent benefit for the right policyholder.

Life settlements are unfamiliar to most people, but they can have excellent financial returns depending on the time the policy is held. The insurance company also guarantees that the proceeds will be paid at the time of death, which limits, but does not remove the financial risk.

Art

Full disclosure: I have never understood art. I remember attending a party in a mansion in Dallas when I was a medical student. The powder room had an original Picasso hanging over the commode. I was impressed but couldn't understand why that little picture was worth so much. I failed to comprehend that fine art is a great way to hold wealth.

Author Jim Rickards has said that financial dynasties of the past held their wealth in real estate, gold, and fine art. All I know is that every time a famous painting is sold, it seems to bring a higher price than before.

If you have a penchant for art and the funds to invest, this can be a legitimate method to preserve wealth. I have even read that art can produce passive income when it's leased to a gallery. So lease your Monet to an art gallery and your troubles are over!

Philanthropy

Giving money to worthwhile causes activates the reward center in your brain, makes you feel good, improves your community, and creates a good public image. It can also have a positive effect on your tax situation. Tacked on to all the worthwhile benefits of philanthropy is the ability to offset as much as 50 percent of your adjustable gross income in any given year; the government provides a tax incentive because it wants to keep charitable giving robust.[65] It's a win-win. You lower your tax burden while improving the lives of those you wish to support. Again, check with your CPA to get proper guidance.

Other Tools

There are plenty of other strategies you can use on your quest for financial independence. These include conservation easements, tax liens, blockchain technology, specially designed retirement plans, hard money lending, and a host of others. As you move through your journey, you'll learn to use some of them while discarding others. They represent a Swiss Army knife of options for financial freedom—you choose the tools that best fit your situation.

Be an Insider

One of the advantages of being wealthy is that opportunities are brought to you—legal "insider" deals—that others will never see or only when it's too late to take advantage. Robert Kiyosaki says that the "I" in the *Cashflow Quadrant* not only stands for Investor but also for "Insider."

As you become skilled in your market and asset class, either as a passive investor, or sponsor, you will instinctively know what constitutes a good deal and what doesn't. Others in the space will know you are knowledgeable about this type of product and will bring you opportunities that others haven't seen yet. You will become an Insider. This is the reward for becoming educated, being patient, and always acting ethically. Good things will come your way and sneak up on you when you aren't looking!

As emphasized throughout this book, there are many ways to create income and wealth. This chapter has given you a taste of what's out there.

You will discover more along your journey. While the vehicles vary, the principles you have learned in this book remain constant and work for all of them.

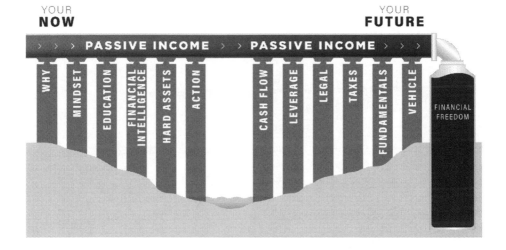

BUILDING YOUR
PASSIVE INCOME PIPELINE

Build a Pipeline to Your Dreams

It is only the farmer who faithfully plants seeds in the spring,
who reaps a harvest in the autumn.

—BC FORBES

I recently attended a medical conference dinner where I had the pleasure of meeting an engaging 80-year-old orthopedic surgeon. He had a wealth of experience and I enjoyed picking his brain about the "old days." We were having a great conversation about medicine and money when he said something that startled me and sent chills up my spine. "I have been married to my second wife for 37 years and she has always been by my side," he said. "She should not have to worry about every penny that goes out of the house!"

Apparently, at age 80, he was still working as a full-time surgeon. He said that after fifty years he still enjoyed his work, but he was working out of necessity, not choice. I did not dig deeper because it wasn't my place, but his comments made my heart heavy.

If it was possible, I would have gone back in time and told him to invest in cash-flowing hard assets that would produce passive income so that when he did reach 80, money wouldn't be a worry. I wanted to tell his younger self about personal development, tax strategies, leverage, and how money could work for him rather than the other way around. I desperately wanted him to know the joy of financial freedom when he most deserved it! Sadly, time machines don't exist. I couldn't help him now.

We all have choices in life, and the doctor I spoke to that day may have made good or bad ones. We'll never know. But the thing to realize is that his situation doesn't have to be *your* future. If you've made it this far in the book—and I'm grateful if you have—then at least you've chosen to educate yourself and pursue financial freedom. Bravo! Your future is bright! But don't stop there. Education is good, but it's empty without action.

In general, the first priority is to decide what "the life of your dreams" looks like. In other words, "Why do you want to be a rich doctor." Then decide what it will take to make you feel—pardon the cliché—wealthy and wise. This might include some personal development to examine your current mindset and determine if an upgrade is required. After that, you will need to be educated about how to reach your goal, just like you did for medicine. You will learn that it's not how much money you make but how you make your money.

After setting this groundwork, it will be time to act. You must get in the game! Start small but start. Be prepared for roadblocks and setbacks. They will make you stronger and they will teach you the greatest lessons. As you gain knowledge and experience, you will learn to use leverage to speed up your progress. Part of your leverage will be working with professionals who will help you pay less in taxes and protect you from unexpected surprises such as lawsuits.

Soon you will be talking in the language of your chosen path, and eventually, you'll become an expert. You will realize that the tools available to the wealthiest people are available to you as well. As you use those tools and the education you've amassed to create the life you want, you may decide to give back to your community in some way. I leave that up to you.

In closing, I would like to share with you a story that is reprinted here, with permission, from Robert Kiyosaki's *Cashflow Quadrant*. It encapsulates one of the most critical themes of this book.

"Once upon a time there was this quaint little village. It was a great place to live except for one problem. The village had no water unless it rained. To solve this problem once and for all, the village elders decided to put out to bid the contract to have water delivered to the village on a daily basis. Two people volunteered to take on the task and the elders awarded the contract to both of them. They felt that a little competition would keep prices low and insure a backup supply of water.

"The first of the two people who won the contract, Ed, immediately ran out, bought two galvanized steel buckets and began running back and forth along the trail to the lake which was a mile away. He immediately began making money as he labored morning to dusk hauling water from the lake with his two buckets. He would empty them into the large concrete holding tank the village had built. Each morning he had to get up before the rest of the village awoke to make sure there was enough water for the village when it wanted it. It was hard work, but he was very happy to be making money and for having one of the two exclusive contracts for this business.

"The second winning contractor, Bill, disappeared for a while. He was not seen for months, which made Ed very happy since he had no competition. Ed was making all the money.

"Instead of buying two buckets to compete with Ed, Bill had written a business plan, created a corporation, found four investors, employed a president to do the work, and returned six months later with a construction crew. Within a year his team had built a large-volume stainless steel pipeline which connected the village to the lake.

"At the grand opening celebration, Bill announced that his water was cleaner than Ed's water. Bill knew that there had been complaints about dirt in Ed's water. Bill also announced that he could supply the village with water 24 hours a day, seven days a week. Ed could only deliver water on the weekdays... he did not work on weekends. Then Bill announced that he would charge 75 percent less than Ed did for this higher-quality and more reliable

source of water. The village cheered and ran immediately for the faucet at the end of Bill's pipeline.

"In order to compete, Ed immediately lowered his rates by 75 percent, bought two more buckets, added covers to his buckets, and began hauling four buckets each trip. In order to provide better service, he hired his two sons to give him a hand for the night shift and on weekends. When his boys went off to college, he said to them, 'Hurry back because someday this business will belong to you.'

"For some reason, after college, his two sons never returned. Eventually Ed had employee and union problems. The union was demanding higher wages, better benefits, and wanted its members to only haul one bucket at a time.

"Bill, on the other hand, realized that if this village needed water, then other villages must need water too. He rewrote his business plan and went off to sell his high-speed, high-volume, low-cost, and clean water delivery system to villages throughout the world. He only makes a penny per bucket of water delivered, but he delivers billions of buckets of water every day. Regardless if he works or not, billions of people consume billions of buckets of water, and all that money pours into his bank account. Bill had developed a pipeline to deliver money to himself as well as water to the villages.

"Bill lived happily ever after and Ed worked hard for the rest of his life and had financial problems forever after.

"The end."

The "Pipeline Story" was created by Robert Kiyosaki in his bestselling book, Rich Dad's CASHFLOW Quadrant: Guide to Financial Freedom. To learn more go to www.richdad. com. Used with permission of CASHFLOW Technologies, Inc. All rights reserved. This grant of permission is not an endorsement of Tom Burns, or the content of this book.

Back in the good old days, hauling buckets worked for doctors. Our buckets were big and shiny, and they carried more water than we could ever need. Thus, we were able to save the excess and live off it for the rest of our lives. Now our buckets are small, rusty, and leaky. We must carry more buckets every day just to keep up. What will we do when we're too old to carry buckets?

Now, close your eyes and imagine preparing breakfast for your children every morning, then having all the time in the world to play with them after school. Picture yourself on the vacation of your dreams, every other month! Visualize a stress-free medical practice in which you are caring for your fellow man without concern for your income or survival. Play the movie of your ideal life with the soothing sounds of your pipeline running in the background.

Rich doctors don't haul buckets and they don't work for money. They build pipelines of passive income, enjoy extraordinary lives, and create the freedom to pursue what is most meaningful to them and the world around them.

Enjoy the journey!
Tom

References

Chapter 1:

Chapter 2:
1. Medscape National Physician Burnout, Depression & Suicide Report 2019. https://www.medscape.com/slideshow/2019-lifestyle-burnout-depression-6011056#5
2. Peckham, C. (2018, January 17). Medscape Physician Burnout & Depression Report 2018. Retrieved from https://www.medscape.com/slideshow/2018-lifestyle-burnout-depression-6009235
3. Budd, K. (2018, October 9). 7 Ways to reduce medical school debt. *AAMC News*. Retrieved from https://news.aamc.org/medical-education/article/7-ways-reduce-medical-school-debt/

Chapter 3:
4. The Highest Paying Jobs of 2018. *Glassdoor*. https://www.glassdoor.com/blog/highest-paying-jobs-2018/

Chapter 4:
5. U.S. Physicians—Statistics & Facts. Retrieved from https://www.statista.com/topics/1244/physicians/
6. U.S. and World Population Clock Census Bureau. https://www.census.gov/popclock/
7. Lally, P. et al, (2009, July 16). How are habits formed: Modelling habit formation in the real world. Abstract. *European Journal of Social Psychology*. Retrieved from http://www.onlinelibrary.wiley.com
8. Vifredo Pareto. https://www.toolshero.com/toolsheroes/vilfredo-pareto/
9. Pareto principle: Definition and meaning. *Business Dictionary*. www.businessdictionary.com/definition/Pareto-principle.html

Chapter 5:
10. The Rockefeller Foundation. A Digital History. https://rockfound.rockarch.org/general_education_board
11. Griffin, GE. *The Creature From Jekyll Island*. American Media, 2010.
12. General Education Board, Occasional Papers, No. 1. (General Education Board, New York, 1913) p. 6.

13. Lee, SJ and Reeves, TC. (2018). Chapter 7. Edgar Dale and the Cone of Experience. Retrieved from https://lidtfoundations.pressbooks.com/chapter/edgar-dale-and-the-cone-of-experience/
14. Edison. I have gotten a lot of results! *Quote Investigator.* https://quoteinvestigator.com/2012/07/31/edison-lot-results/
15. Willis, J., & Todorov, A. (2006). *First Impressions: Making Up Your Mind After a 100-Ms Exposure to a Face. Psychological Science*, 17(7), 592–598. https://doi.org/10.1111/j.1467-9280.2006.01750.x
16. Neil Howlett, Karen Pine, Ismail Orakçıoğlu, Ben Fletcher, (2013) "The influence of clothing on first impressions: Rapid and positive responses to minor changes in male attire", *Journal of Fashion Marketing and Management: An International Journal*, Vol. 17 Issue: 1, pp.38-48, https://doi.org/10.1108/13612021311305128

Chapter 6:

17. Bryan, K. (2016, August 17) Research shows 60% of Americans are spending all or more than their income: https://americasavesweek.org/research-shows-60-of-americans-are-spending-all-or-more-than-their-income/
18. Rickards, J. *Strategic Intelligence.* April 2018. www.agorafinancial.com
19. Royal, J and O'Shea, A. (2019, May 15). What is the Average Stock Market Return? [Web log post]. Retrieved from https://www.nerdwallet.com/blog/investing/average-stock-market-return/
20. McMahon, T. (2014, April 1) Long-Term U.S. Inflation. [Web log post] Retrieved from https://inflationdata.com/inflation/inflation_rate/long_term_inflation.asp
21. Daily Capital. (2014, July 28). Hidden 401k Fees Are Costing You A Fortune: Here's What You Could Do With The Money. [Web log post]. Retrieved from https://www.personalcapital.com/blog/investing/hidden-401k-fees-costing-fortune/
22. Enron files for bankruptcy. *History.* (2018, August 21). https://www.history.com/this-day-in-history/enron-files-for-bankruptcy
23. La Monica, PR. (2001, November 29). Where Wall Street went wrong. *CNNMoney.* Retrieved from https://money.cnn.com/2001/11/29/investing/q_enronanalysts
24. Yang, S. (2014, July 1). 5 Years Ago Bernie Madoff Was Sentenced to 150 Years in Prison—Here's How His Scheme Worked. *Business Insider.* https://www.businessinsider.com/how-bernie-madoffs-ponzi-scheme-worked-2014-7
25. Bernard Madoff Fast Facts. CNN Library. (2019, April 22). https://www.cnn.com/2013/03/11/us/bernard-madoff-fast-facts/index.html
26. Christ, C. (2018, June 11). Reuters Health. *Young surgeons face high debt, financial instability.* Retrieved from https://www.reuters.com/article/us-health-surgeons-debt/young-surgeons-face-high-debt-financial-instability-idUSKBN1J7248

Chapter 7:

27. Nixon Ends Convertibility of US Dollars to Gold and Announces Wage/Price Controls. *Federal Reserve History.* https://www.federalreservehistory.org/essays/gold_convertibility_ends

28. The Great Recession. *Federal Reserve History.* https://www.federalreservehistory.org/essays/great_recession_of_200709

29. The Fed—What is the purpose of the Federal Reserve System? https://www.federalreserve.gov/faqs/about_12594.htm

30. U.S. Bureau of Labor Statistics, Consumer Price Index for All Urban Consumers: Purchasing Power of the Consumer Dollar [CUUR0000SA0R]. Retrieved from FRED, Federal Reserve Bank of St. Louis; https://fred.stlouisfed.org/series/CUUR0000SA0R Retrieved February 9, 2020.

31. The 1923 hyperinflation. Alpha History. https://alphahistory.com/weimarrepublic/1923-hyperinflation/

32. Hanke, S. Hyperinflation in Zimbabwe. The Cato Institute https://www.cato.org/zimbabwe

33. *Farmers' Almanac. A Look Back At What Things Used To Cost—Yesterday and Today.* https://www.farmersalmanac.com/a-look-back-at-what-things-used-to-cost-18228

34. Cherf, J. (2017, October). *Unsustainable Physician Reimbursement Rates.* American Academy of Orthopedic Surgeons, AAOS Now. Retrieved from https://www.aaos.org/aaosnow/2017/oct/cover/cover01/

35. SBA Office of Advocacy. FAQ's. https://www.sba.gov/sites/default/files/FAQ_Sept_2012.pdf

36. Survival Rates and Firm Age. Small Business Administration. https://www.sba.gov/sites/default/files/SurvivalRatesAndFirmAge_ADA_0_0.pdf

37. Babe Ruth jersey sells for record $4.4 million. Espn.com. www.espn.com/mlb/story/_/id/7953437/babe-ruth-jersey-sells-record-44-million

38. Steve Cohen buys Picasso'e *Le Reve* for $155 million. Theartwolf.com www.theartwolf.com/news/picasso-reve-sold-cohen.htm

39. Yakowicz, W. (2019, February 10). *How The World's Billionaires Got So Rich. Forbes.* Retrieved from https://www.forbes.com/sites/willyakowicz/2019/03/09/how-the-worlds-billionaires-got-so-rich/

40. Mercado, D. (2018, September 12). Here's how some of the wealthiest people are investing their cash. Retrieved from https://cnb.cx/2P83HX1

41. Glass, A (2013, July 8). Dow Jones falls to its lowest point, July 8, 1932. https://www.politico.com/story/2013/07/this-day-in-politics-july-8-1932-093787

42. Stock Market Crash of 1987. Federal Reserve History. https://www.federalreservehistory.org/essays/stock_market_crash_of_1987

43. 11 historic bear markets. *NBC News.* www.nbcnews.com/id/37740147/ns/business-stocks_and.../t/historic-bear-markets/

44. (2020, March 17). The Dow's biggest single-day gains and losses in history. *Fox Business.* https://www.foxbusiness.com/markets/the-dows-biggest-single-day-drops-in-history.

Chapter 8:

Chapter 9:

45. Occupational Outlook Handbook, *Bureau of Labor Statistics*. https://www.bls.gov/ooh/construction-and-extraction/carpenters.htm

46. Orthopedic Surgeon Salary in the United States. *Salary.com* https://www.salary.com/research/salary/alternate/orthopedic-surgeon-hourly-wages

Chapter 10:

Chapter 11:

47. Writer873. (2012, January 18). *The Great Pyramid of Giza: Last Remaining Wonder of the Ancient. Ancient History Encyclopedia.* Retrieved from https://www.ancient.eu/article/124/the-great-pyramid-of-gixa-last-remaining-wonder-of/

48. No Author. *Khufu's Great Pyramid.* Retrieved from http://www.unmuseum.org/kpyramid.htm

49. 500dollarmillionaire. Henry Ford was the Smartest ignorant man in history. *500 Dollar Millionaire.* https://500dollarmillionaire.wordpress.com/2013/06/26/henry-ford-was-the-smartest-ignorant-man-in-history/

Chapter 12:

50. Phillips, R and Wamhoff, S. The Federal Estate Tax: An Important Progressive Revenue Source. Institute on Taxation and Economic Policy. https://itep.org/the-federal-estate-tax-an-important-progressive-revenue-source/

Chapter 13:

51. Farley, R. (2012, August 3). Does Romney Pay a Lower Rate in Taxes Than You? Retrieved from https://www.factcheck.org/2012/08/does-romney-pay-a-lower-rate-in-taxes-than-you/

52. Trump: I'm 'smart' for paying no taxes—YouTube. https://www.youtube.com/watch?v=-qXjsMK_MnU

53. Helvering v. Gregory, 69 F.2d 809 (2d Cir. 1934)—Justia Law. https://law.justia.com/cases/federal/appellate-courts/F2/69/809/1562063/

54. Elkins, K. (2018, March 2). 12 countries that pay less in taxes than the US. Retrieved from https://www.cnbc.com/2018/03/02/countries-that-pay-less-in-taxes-than-the-us.html

55. Chris. (2018, November 21). Countries Without Income Tax. *Globalization Guide.* Retrieved from https://globalisationguide.org/countries-without-income-tax/

56. Ironman. (2014, April 11). How Many Pages in the U.S. Tax Code? *Business Insider.* Retrieved from https://www.businessinsider.com/2014-how-many-pages-in-the-us-tax-code-2014-4

57. What Is a 1031 Tax Exchange? The Basics for Real Estate Investors. *CWS Capital Partners LLC.* https://www.cwscapital.com/what-is-a-1031-exchange/ (Retrieved March 2018)

58. Top 3 Tax Benefits of Oil and Gas Investing. *Energy Funders*. https://www.energyfunders.com/blog/oil-investing-benefits/

59. H.R.3838—99th Congress (1985-1986): Tax Reform Act of 1986. https://www.congress.gov/bill/99th-congress/house-bill/3838

Chapter 14:

Chapter 15:

60. Yakowicz, W. (2019, February 10). *How The World's Billionaires Got So Rich. Forbes.* Retrieved from https://www.forbes.com/sites/willyakowicz/2019/03/09/how-the-worlds-billionaires-got-so-rich/

61. Mercado, D. (2018, September 12). Here's how some of the wealthiest people are investing their cash. Retrieved from https://cnb.cx/2P83HX1

62. Harry Dent Details his Forecast for Gold. Retrieved from YouTube, Nov 16, 2018. https://www.youtube.com/watch?v=G-1e-rLNt5Q

63. Jim Rickards: $10,000 Gold is Coming. Retrieved from YouTube, August 8, 2019. https://www.youtube.com/watch?v=EEZ2ZZVKBzE

64l Agrawal, AJ. (2016, February 2). 5 Assets Wealthy People Use to Preserve Wealth. Retrieved from https://www.inc.com/aj-agrawal/5-assets-wealthy-people-use-to-preserve-wealth.html

65. Dickler, J. (2017, October 12). The tax advantages of charitable giving. Retrieved from https://www.cnbc.com/2017/10/12/the-tax-advantages-of-charitable-giving.html

About the Author

Photo courtesy of David Lubin

om Burns is an orthopedic surgeon in Austin, Texas, and a physician for the U.S. Ski Team. He is a co-founder of Presario Ventures, a real estate private equity company headquartered in Austin, Texas. He is also the founder of RichDoctor. com, a website designed to help physicians achieve financial independence.

His mission is to improve health care by helping to create an army of financially free doctors who will continue to care for people with the passion that first drew them to medicine.

He is a seasoned real estate professional and, in conjunction with his partners, manages hundreds of millions of dollars of real estate assets for himself and his investors. He is a popular speaker, frequent podcast guest, and a writer for nationally circulated print media.

Tom splits his time between Austin and Steamboat Springs, Colorado. He enjoys travel to exotic locations and is most comfortable in the wilderness. He spends his time with his wife of 36 years, his two children, and anyone who strives to be a better version of themselves.

True wealth isn't created by living within your means; it's produced by expanding your means.

Expand your means and join Tom on his adventures while he discusses medicine, money, real estate and travel through his personal blogs and videos.

Email hello@richdoctor.com for details.

Your life is a mirror of your thoughts, so if you want to change your situation, you can't do it with the same thoughts that got you to where you are today.

Connect with Rich Doctor

Congratulations on finishing the book! Wherever you are on your journey to financial wealth, it doesn't stop here. In order to create freedom, you must continue to grow and evolve.

We're all in this together, and I want to help you achieve your goals. If more of us create the freedom that we desire, then there will be more of us to produce true change in the world.

Join the Rich Doctor Community
Go to: www.richdoctor.com

There you will have access to supportive content and resources, designed to help us all reach our true potential. As times change, so will the information. What won't change is our connection to each other and our desire to create abundant lives for ourselves and those around us.

Nobody does it alone, and it is my mission to provide resources and community for doctors that wish to live life financially free.

Visit **www.richdoctor.com** today and continue your journey to true wealth and freedom.

RichDoctor

Freedom Through Passive Income

www.richdoctor.com | hello@richdoctor.com